The Experimenter's A–Z of Mathematics

Maths Activities with Computer Support

Steve Humble

David Fulton Publishers

London

David Fulton Publishers Ltd
Ormond House, 26–27 Boswell Street, London WC1N 3JZ

www.fultonpublishers.co.uk

First published 2002

British Library Cataloguing in Publication Data
A catalogue record for this book is available from the British Library

ISBN 1–85346–817–7

Typeset by Kate Williams, Abergavenny
Printed in Great Britain by Bell and Bain Ltd, Glasgow

Contents

To those for whom the path's not clear.

The path's not clear.
Is it left or right?
It needs more work
To find it out.

There're many behind us
With a point of view
But they don't know
What to do.

The puzzle goes on
Day and night.
The path's not clear
But it's always right.

Steve Humble 2001

Thank you, Linda, Daniel and Matthew, for all your help.

Introduction: What is Mathematics?

Mathematical knowledge plays a key part in our basic human desire to understand more. It offers tools to expand our knowledge of the world around us, helping our understanding of everything from counting to the cosmic structure of the universe. Its impact on our culture cannot be understated, as without mathematical knowledge there would have been few technical revolutions. Electricity is one such revolution which would not have been developed if it were not for the mathematical genius of James Clerk Maxwell. In 1860 he combined the laws of electricity and magnetism with the laws of the behaviour of light. His equations defining this union stand as a testament to mankind's quest to know more.

Yet mathematics is an ability to see more than just laws; it is the development of our logical mind. As Paul Dirac said, 'I understand what an equation means if I have a way of figuring out the characteristics of its solution without actually solving it.' Dirac is saying that before he would try to solve the equation, he would experiment by putting some numbers into the equation, or by doing some algebra. He would spend some time getting to know the equation by playing with it before he would attempt to solve it. This experimental stage in our understanding of new ideas is very important, since it gives us time to think about the problem and find out some of its properties.

The history of mathematics gives you an insight into how great mathematicians in the past have experimented with the subject. This is an area of mathematics that I feel is sometimes lost sight of in its teaching. As teachers we stand in the middle of all that has gone before and all that is to come, so in teaching the young we have a role to play in the history of mathematics, which is a history full of interesting characters, all of whom have their stories to tell. I have made it a habit during my teaching career to collect these tales whenever I happen upon them. Each chapter in the book starts with a story that gives an interesting introduction to the topic and thereby captures the student's imagination, giving the problem some real-life focus. Students sometimes ask me why we study a particular topic; the history of mathematics can usually supply an answer.

I remember, years ago, watching a *Horizon* programme about Richard Feynman, the American Nobel-prize winning physicist. He was talking about a little problem he worked on, but first he told a story. 'I was sitting in the cafeteria in Cornell University and some lad threw a Frisbee into the air. The pattern in the center seemed to go around faster than the wobbling.' He then went to his office and, in a few hours, worked out that the ratio of the rotation to the wobble was 1:2. He said the result came out of solving some equations. This story made me wonder whether I could solve this problem, so I tried, but made little progress. My mechanics knowledge of this type of problem at the time was not that good. I worked on the problem for a year, on and off – not all the time, as I was teaching and doing other things! I read lots of books, and by the end of the year I could solve the problem. It was a messy sort of solution, but a solution just the same. Another year passed and my interest in mechanical problems grew, and, of course, I read more books. One day, while sitting at my desk, I suddenly thought of a different way to solve the problem. I had not worked on the wobbling Frisbee problem for at least three months, so I thought at first that my idea may not work. However, after 30 minutes or so I had this lovely solution and I was walking on air. It was such a wonderful feeling to see this beautiful result. I thought back to Feynman and how he had seemed so happy. I understood why.

Peter's method is something you have probably not heard of unless you were in class 9G on the great day when Peter told me about his idea to speed up a calculation we had to make to get answers to an experiment we were doing. I remember it well. 'Sir, I've found this quicker way to get the answer, could you look at it?' Peter struggled with fractions and did not seem to enjoy mathematics, yet while he was telling me his idea I could tell he was excited about his discovery. His method was simple, but good. I asked him to tell the class. He asked me to tell the class, so I did, and I called it Peter's method. The class thought it was great and all used it. After that day Peter changed; his maths improved greatly. The class would sometimes say to him 'Peter, have you got a quick method for this one?' 'I'm working on it,' he would reply.

Mathematics at all levels is about the joy in discovery. It's about finding things out. I have found that an experimental approach to mathematics gives all students this opportunity.

The Experimenter's A–Z of Mathematics is a journey, a path, that twists and turns, looking at a small part of this great subject. I can only say to the giants of the past, whose names I do not have the space to include, that no offence is meant.

Sir Isaac Newton said,

> *I know not what I may seem to the world, but as to myself, I seem to have been only like a boy playing on the sea shore, and diverting myself in now and then finding a smoother pebble or prettier shell than ordinary, whilst the great ocean of truth lay all undiscovered before me.*

What's It All About...?

The Experimenter's A–Z of Mathematics is a book with stories to tell. It can be read from A to Z or you can dip in and out as you wish, since all of the chapters are completely self-contained. Each chapter starts with a story to set the scene for the work to follow. The idea behind this is to capture the student's imagination and thereby give a good introduction to the lesson. The story then leads nicely into a mathematical experiment. I've used these experiments with a variety of age groups all the way up to sixth form. I do not think that there is a set age for experimental investigation in mathematics, as different age groups always ask different questions of the task and search for different levels of answers.

The same can be said of ability. I have found these experiments highly motivating for low-ability students, since the students feel that they can do maths in a mathematics lesson. As for the students at the other end of the ability scale, the book opens up a wide horizon of extension ideas and further reference. Links to websites and further reading are also included at the end of every chapter. All websites listed were accessible at the time of publication. Even the most gifted can be stretched to their limit and beyond.

A computer support section is offered in a number of chapters, offering graphical and numerical output, to allow students to experiment with more complex situations. The CD-ROM contains a Microsoft Excel spreadsheet and a graphics calculator file ready to download into your machine. There are also BASIC code files which will run in a QBASIC environment. QBASIC comes with Windows 95 or 98, or can be downloaded free of charge from any of

http//qball.cjb.net
www.download.com
www.freeware.com
www.cnet.com

QBASIC works much the same as all other packages on your PC. For example, with QBASIC you double click to open it, then use <File> to access the file you want from the CD-ROM. See overleaf for an example. When you click on <OK> you will see the file for the program appear on the screen. Then use <Run> to use the program. It is useful to know that pressing <CTRL>+<BREAK> at any stage will stop the program running and take you back to the file. From then on instructions are given on the screen. For further information on the experiment that uses RAMAN see Chapter R.

The programs do not have a fancy interface as they have been written with the intention of allowing the user to edit lines of the files if required.

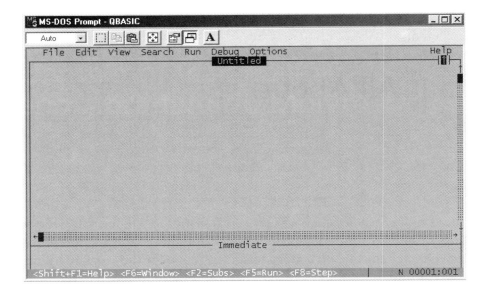

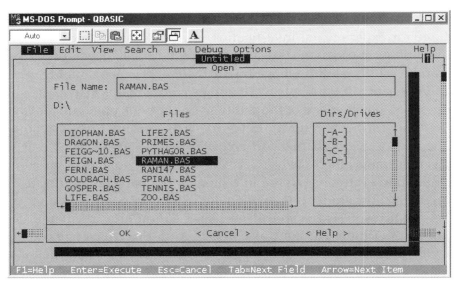

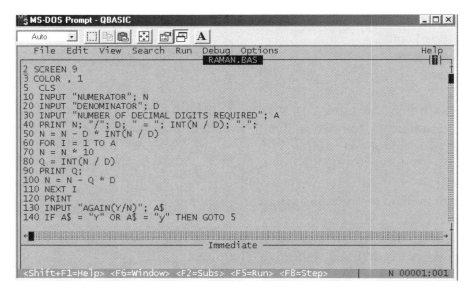

The Computer support section in the ICT chapters merely does what it says, and offers support. By systematically changing a few numbers students can enjoy experimenting and making discoveries in high-level mathematical problems. The story goes that Gauss was very interested in prime numbers and used to spend 'an idle quarter of an hour or so to count through another chiliad here and there'. Gauss published a list of the prime numbers up to three million and used this to help with his experiments in prime number theory (see Chapter P). If he had lived now a computer could have made this calculation in a few minutes. It makes you wonder about how much more these great mathematicians of the past could have discovered with the help of computer support!

A Algebra and Descartes

Al-Khwarizmi is credited with the invention of algebraic notational methods in 820AD. In his most important book, *Al-jabr wa'l muqābalah* (from the title of which the word 'algebra' was derived), he solves quadratic equations in a way that would not be familiar to our students, using a method that is much the same as that used by computer programmers to write code for their programs. His method follows a set of logical instructions to obtain the answer. This type of method is called an algorithm, from the Latin corruption of his name, *algorismus*.

It was not until the sixteenth century that the idea of algebraic methods really took hold and mathematicians started to solve equations using the rules of algebra that we use today. New symbols then started to appear with daunting regularity in newly published papers. Today there are literally thousands of symbols in mathematical notation. How do our students react to these symbols? Some react very badly, and this leads to problems in their future understanding. Others love the eccentric element of the secret code that is mathematics. They rise to the challenge and become passionately involved in trying to crack the code in order to solve problems.

In 1545, Nicolo Tartaglia (Nicolo of Brescia) managed to solve some problems of the form $x^3 + mx^2 = n$, and he was very pleased with his discovery. His general solution is

$$x = \left[\frac{n}{2} + \sqrt{\left(\frac{n}{2}\right)^2 + \left(\frac{m}{3}\right)^3} \right]^{\frac{1}{3}} - \left[-\frac{n}{2} + \sqrt{\left(\frac{n}{2}\right)^2 + \left(\frac{m}{3}\right)^3} \right]^{\frac{1}{3}}$$

This news soon spread to Girolamo Cardano, who was soon to publish a book on algebra (*Ars magna*) and thought that this would make a good chapter in his new book. He invited Tartaglia to come and tell him of his methods, which he did. History is soon rewritten, and today it is Cardano who is credited in most history books with the solution to these equations. But the twist was yet to come.

The Arab mathematician Al-Khwarizmi (800–850), as featured on a stamp published in the Soviet Union in 1983

Girolamo Cardano (1501–1576)

Tartaglia's solution was so good that it went beyond the mathematical knowledge of the day.

For example, consider the equation $x^3 - 15x = 4$, which has $x = 4$ as a solution. You can see that this is the solution by substituting 4 into the equation to give $4^3 - 15 \times 4 = 4$. Yet when Cardano used the formula it gave this strange answer:

$$x = \left(2 + \sqrt{-121}\right)^{\frac{1}{3}} - \left(-2 + \sqrt{-121}\right)^{\frac{1}{3}}$$

In his book, Cardano gives a calculation method to avoid this type of problem, but it is clear that he does not really understand what is happening in this case. It would, in fact, take a further 200 years of mathematics until we could see that this is a complex solution, which can be solved to give the correct answer. Cardano unwittingly and without understanding stumbled on the future. Our understanding of mathematical algebra continues to grow to this day. There are still a vast number of equations that cannot be solved and we are waiting for future methods to unlock their secrets.

René Descartes (1596–1650) was a very great mathematician. In his book *The Rules for the Direction of the Mind* he presents a universal method for the solution of problems. It comes down to three basic steps.

1. Reduce any kind of problem to a mathematical problem.
2. Reduce any kind of mathematical problem to a problem of algebra.
3. Reduce any problem of algebra to the solution of a single equation.

For some problems these steps become very difficult, if not impossible, yet in school mathematics they are often a good scheme to follow when solving problems. The only additional step that proves useful is a certain amount of experimenting, which helps all children get a feel for the problem since it takes away some of the fear generated by strange symbols.

Experiment time

The following algebraic problems can be made more accessible to students by using an experimental approach before you start on the Descartes method. This will give the students time to become familiar with the problem, and understand the reasons for using algebraic symbols.

Problem 1

A farmer keeps hens and rabbits. Altogether, his animals have 50 heads and 140 feet. How many hens and rabbits does the farmer have?

Trial and improvement

Could they all be hens? No, as they would only have 100 feet.
Could they all be rabbits? No, because they would have 200 feet.
What about half and half?
This method will eventually produce the answer.

The Descartes method

Using the Descartes method we would write down some algebra. The number of hens is represented by x, and the number of rabbits by y. Using this notation gives the following equations:

50 heads gives $\qquad x + y = 50$

140 feet gives $\qquad 2x + 4y = 140$

We are now in stage 2 and can move to stage 3 by solving these simultaneous equations to give $y = 20$ and $x = 30$. So the farmer has 30 hens and 20 rabbits.

Problem 2

Water enters an empty tank through three pipes. The water entering through one pipe can fill a tank in 15 minutes, entering through the second pipe it can fill it in 20 minutes, and entering through the third pipe it can fill it in 30 minutes. With water entering through all three pipes, how long will it take to fill the empty tank?

First, by experiment, we can get a feel for the whole problem. Let us assume that the tank fills with 100 litres of water. How much water would enter the tank in 1 minute? There would be $\left(\frac{1}{15} + \frac{1}{20} + \frac{1}{30}\right) \times 100 = 15$ litres in 1 minute. So clearly you need more time.

How much water would be in the tank after 4 minutes?

There would be $\left(\frac{4}{15} + \frac{4}{20} + \frac{4}{30}\right) \times 100 = 60$ litres, and so the experiment develops.

You can see how the whole idea of experimenting builds understanding of the problem.

We need to make an assumption at the start of this problem that the tank will contain x litres of water when it is full. Then the amount of water flowing through the first pipe per minute is $\frac{x}{15}$ litres. In t minutes, the amount of water that would have flowed through the first pipe is $\frac{x}{15}t$. When using all three pipes you get $\frac{x}{15}t + \frac{x}{20}t + \frac{x}{30}t = x$. To solve this equation and find t, you first divide out the x's, then simplify to get $t = 6\frac{2}{3}$ minutes.

Experimenting at the start of this more difficult problem may not find the answer, but will help to give the students a greater understanding of the method used.

Problem 2 is in the same mode as the classic work problems. In Problem 3 I reword Problem 2 to show how these sorts of questions can be solved.

Problem 3

Tom can do a job in 15 hours, Dick in 20 hours, and Harry in 30 hours. If they do the job together how long does it take to complete the job?

This is the same as Problem 2, so the equation to solve is $\frac{t}{15} + \frac{t}{20} + \frac{t}{30} = 1$.

Problem 4

'The Cattle and the Sun' is a great algebraic problem created by Archimedes, who is famous for shouting 'Eureka!' in the bath. It is a very difficult algebraic problem which has only recently been fully solved, yet there are still many parts of it that are accessible to students. My students enjoy trying to form the equations given in the letter sent by Archimedes to Eratosthenes in 244BC. They can also verify that the solution is correct. Some students become so fascinated by the problem that they try to solve the seven equations themselves.

The Greek mathematician Archimedes (c.287–212BC)

Here is the translated letter:

> *The sun god had a herd of cattle consisting of bulls and cows, one part of which was white, a second black, a third spotted, and a fourth brown.*
>
> *Among the bulls, the number of white ones was one half plus one third the number of the black greater than the brown; the number of the black, one quarter plus one fifth the number of the spotted greater than the brown; the number of the spotted, one sixth plus one seventh the number of the white greater than the brown.*
>
> *Among the cows, the number of white ones was one third plus one quarter of the total black cattle; the number of the black, one quarter plus one fifth the total of the spotted cattle; the number of the spotted, one fifth plus one sixth the total of the brown cattle; the number of the brown, one sixth plus one seventh the total of the white cattle.*
>
> *What was the composition of the herd?*

Using the symbols:

	Bulls	Cows
White	A	a
Black	B	b
Brown	C	c
Spotted	D	d

the seven equations can be written as follows:

$$A - C = \tfrac{5}{6}B \qquad a = \tfrac{7}{12}(B + b)$$
$$B - C = \tfrac{9}{20}D \qquad b = \tfrac{9}{20}(D + d)$$
$$D - C = \tfrac{13}{42}A \qquad c = \tfrac{13}{42}(A + a)$$
$$\qquad\qquad\qquad d = \tfrac{11}{30}(C + c)$$

Solving these gives the following answers:

	Bulls	Cows
White	10 366 482	7 206 360
Black	7 460 514	4 893 246
Brown	4 149 387	5 439 213
Spotted	7 358 060	3 515 820

This is the smallest known solution, yet any integer multiple of this is also a solution. Using the above numbers, students can verify that these are true solutions. This turns out to be a fairly difficult task and great care is needed not to make any calculation errors.

In the original problem set by Archimedes, this is only the first part. The letter for this first part ends with the line

thou wouldst not be called unskilled or ignorant of numbers, but not yet shalt thou be numbered among the wise.

The letter then goes on to add two more equations to the seven above. The solution to all nine equations turns out to be incredibly difficult. It was not until 1981 that a solution was found by Harry Nelson using a Cray 1 supercomputer. The answer is so big that it takes 47 sheets of A4 paper to print it out. It seems very unlikely that Archimedes would have been able to solve this problem in his day, due to the size of the numbers involved.

The extra equations are $A + B =$ is a square number and $C + D =$ is a triangular number. The letter then concludes

If thou art able, O stranger, to find out all these things and gather them together in your mind, giving all the relations, thou shalt depart crowned with glory and knowing that thou hast been adjudged perfect in species of wisdom.

For a complete statement of the original letter and solution see www.mcs.drexel.edu/~crorres/archimedes/cattle/statement.html (accessed Oct. 2001) and www.andrews.edu/~calkins/profess/cattle.htm (accessed Oct. 2001).

Extension ideas

Some of the great mathematicians that we will meet later in this book have spent time constructing classic word problems. Here are just a few to give your students brain ache and fun all at once. This is mathematics at its best for school children: that great confusion in their heads saying what is going on, then that great elation when they find the answer. *Warning. He who starts to solve these beware: there is only confusion and madness ahead!*

1. **Euler:** A father who has three sons leaves them 1600 crowns. The will precises, that the eldest shall have 200 crowns more than the second, and the second shall have 100 crowns more than the youngest. Required the share of each.

2. **Newton:** Three workmen can do a piece of work in certain times. A once in 3 weeks, B thrice in 8 weeks, and C five times in 12 weeks. It is desired to know in what time they can finish it jointly.

3. **Fibonacci:** The triangle with sides a, a, and b is isosceles. Cut off from it two triangles, symmetric to each other with respect to the altitude perpendicular to the base b, so that the remaining symmetric pentagon is equilateral. Express the side x of the pentagon in terms of a and b.

4. **Diophantine:** A coiner has three kinds of silver, the first of 7 ounces, the second of 5½ ounces, the third of 4½ ounces fine per marc (a marc is 8 ounces) and he wishes to form a mixture of the weight of 30 marcs at 6 ounces fine per marc: how many marcs of each sort must he take? *Hint: the Diophantine equations to solve are $x + y + z = 30$ and $14x + 11y + 9z = 360$. There are only five integer solutions.*

5. **Whewell:** Represent each of the first 25 natural numbers using exactly four nines, any of the four basic operations (addition, subtraction, multiplication and division), and if absolutely necessary, allowing $\sqrt{9} = 3$. In his correspondence with Michael Faraday, Whewell coined the terms anode, cathode and ion.

6. **Srinivasa Ramanujan** established the following algebraic identities:

    (a) $(a + 1)(b + 1)(c + 1) + (a - 1)(b - 1)(c - 1) \equiv 2(a + b + c + abc)$

    (b) Provided that $a + b + c = 0$ then $a^4 + b^4 + c^4 \equiv 2(ab + bc + ca)^2$

    Show that these are true.

7. **Bachet:** Given a scale with two pans, determine the least number of weights and the values of the weights in order to weigh all integral weights from 1 to 40.

8. **Pythagoras:** A reciprocal triple (a, b, c) has the property that $\left(\frac{1}{a}\right)^2 + \left(\frac{1}{b}\right)^2 = \left(\frac{1}{c}\right)^2$. Show that $(80, 60, 48)$ is a reciprocal triple. Find others.

9. **Conway:** An nth order zigzag number is an arrangement of the digits 1, 2, 3, 4, . . ., n in such a manner that they alternately rise and fall. For example, the only first and second order zigzag numbers are 1 and 12, respectively. There are two third order zigzag numbers, 231 and 132. There are five fourth order zigzag numbers: 3412, 1423, 2413, 1324 and 2314. Determine the 16 fifth order zigzag numbers.

10. **Levy:** Paul Levy conjectured that every odd number greater than 5 can be expressed in the form $2p + q$, where p and q are prime. Show that this is true for all odd numbers between 7 and 49.

11. Can you find the error in the following proof that $1 = 2$?

Let	$a = b$
then	$a \times a = a \times b$
that is	$a^2 = ab$
by subtraction	$a^2 - b^2 = ab - b^2$
factorise to give	$(a - b)(a + b) = b(a - b)$
divide to get	$a + b = b$

    Thus $b + b = b$, since $a = b$, and so $2b = b$ and $2 = 1$

Further references

Boyer, C. and Merzbach, U. C. (1991) *A History of Mathematics*. New York: John Wiley.

Chrystal, G. (1961) *Textbook of Algebra*, 2 vols. New York: Dover. Originally published in two volumes in 1886 and 1899.

Dorrie, H. (1965) *100 Great Problems of Elementary Mathematics: Their History and Solution*, D. Antin (trans.). New York: Dover.

Polya, G. (1990) *How To Solve It*. Harmondsworth: Penguin. Originally published in 1945.

For Archimedes' letter and solution see:
www.mcs.drexel.edu/~crorres/archimedes/cattle/statement.html
www.andrews.edu/~calkins/profess/cattle.htm

B Buffon, Probability and Pi

George-Louis Leclerc, Comte de Buffon, probably raised some eyebrows during his strange experiment in 1777. Imagine the scene in a grand house on what is now Rue Buffon in the Fifth Arrondissement in Paris, the street named after him to honour his development of calculus in probability theory. Buffon is standing in the tiled entrance hall under large chandeliers, throwing loaves of French bread over his shoulder. Servants are running backwards and forwards picking up these loaves, under the careful, if slightly incredulous, gaze of local dignitaries. These dignitaries come from the aristocracy, parliament, church and university. What is Buffon up to now? Buffon is oblivious and continues to throw, counting the number of loaves that touch or cross lines on the floor, and counting the total number of loaves. This is his new theory, and it will give him a place in the history books of mathematics. It is his

The French naturalist George-Louis Leclerc, Comte de Buffon (1707–1788)

special day and he only hears the applause of his peers. Generations of mathematicians to come will use his ideas in many areas of mathematics, including quantum dynamics. Buffon's publicity event not only creates a new theory but gives him a means of estimating π.

Experiment time

Buffon's French loaves created a historic moment in mathematical history, so as you can imagine the theory is not that easy. Let's build our understanding of finding probabilities from areas with a simpler example.

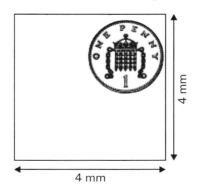

4 mm

4 mm

What is the chance that a coin of diameter 2 cm lies inside a 4 cm square?

This is a game seen at fairgrounds, where you roll a penny on to a grid of squares. If it lies inside the square you win. For it to be inside the square the minimum criterion is that the edge of the coin must just touch the side of the square.

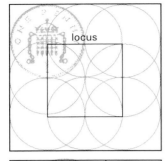

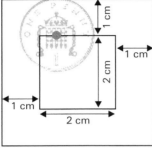

Note that the locus of the centre of the coin forms another square inside the first. As long as the centre of the coin lies somewhere inside this smaller square the coin has to be inside the 4 cm square.

$$\text{probability that a coin is inside the square} = \frac{\text{area of small square}}{\text{area of large square}}$$

$$= \frac{2 \times 2}{4 \times 4} = \frac{4}{16} = \frac{1}{4}$$

For the experiment it is best to use a grid of squares. This avoids bias in the way that the student rolls the coin on to the square. It also means that the student can *roll* the coin on to the grid instead of throwing it into a single square. This will produce a much more random (see Chapter V) effect. The probability that a coin is inside one of the squares on a grid of, say, 20 squares is the same as the probability that the coin is in a single square because you have 20 large and small squares, so the answer can be worked out as:

$$\frac{\text{area of small squares}}{\text{area of large squares}} = \frac{20 \times (2 \times 2)}{20 \times (4 \times 4)} = \frac{80}{320} = \frac{1}{4}$$

To start the experiment it is best to group the students in pairs so that one can roll the coin while the other records the results. They should count the number of times the coin is rolled and the number of times it goes inside the square, checking the probability after 20 and 50 rolls.

$$\text{probability that a coin will be rolled into the square} = \frac{\text{number of coins inside the square}}{\text{number of rolls}}$$

Once each pair has performed the experiment the data from each pair can be combined on the board to find a class result, which will be very close to 0.25.

Now let's see if we can use the coin example to consider the problem of Buffon's loaves.

Buffon's loaves

When you throw a stick on to a grid it does not have complete symmetry and needs to be rotated through 180 degrees to become a circle. This produces the first problem, since each throw of the stick could lie in an infinite number of orientations.

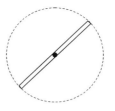

Let us start by looking to see what happens when we take two horizontal parallel lines and a stick which has the same length as the distance between these lines. If the stick falls between them, with its centre at the midpoint between the lines, it can only cross (or touch) the lines at two points, and only when it is vertical.

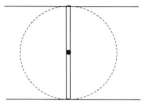

If the stick falls so the centre is slightly higher up (or down) we have an infinite number of crossing points on the line. This diagram shows these, with the shaded area showing the proportion of sticks which would lie on the line when the centre of the stick is at this particular location.

    If we move the centre of the stick higher the number of crossing points would increase and the shaded area would be greater. I have only talked about three cases, but the centre of the stick could be located at an infinite number of points between the two lines. It could cross not only the top line, but also the lower one. You can now start to believe how clever Buffon's idea really is.

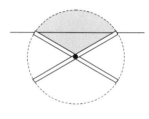

Using the formula for a sector of a circle you can work out one of these areas. I find that students get a better feel for the problems involved when they have carried out this calculation.

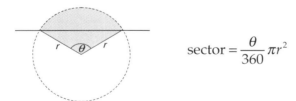

$$\text{sector} = \frac{\theta}{360}\pi r^2$$

So you can see that this situation seems impossible to calculate since how can we add up an infinite number of areas by hand? Buffon's great idea was to add up these areas using calculus.

    When you perform this experiment with the students it is best, as with the coin experiment, to use a grid of squares. The students throw sticks on to the grid, recording the number of throws and the number of times the stick lies on the line.

For a square grid of side a and a stick of length L it can be shown that

$$\text{probability that the stick intersects the line} = \frac{L(4a - L)}{\pi a^2}$$

So with a 4 cm square and a stick of length 2 cm, we have

$$\text{probability that the stick intersects the line } = \frac{2\times(16-2)}{16\pi} = \frac{28}{16\pi} \approx \frac{7}{12}$$

There is also a bonus to this experiment as it gives a means of estimating π. This type of estimating in mathematics is called the Monte Carlo method. See Chapter V for more details on this method. In this case, since π is in the formula for finding the chance that the stick lies on the line, we can treat π as an unknown and solve the equation to find it using our experimental results. For example, in the above case, if you found that the stick crossed the line 29 times in 50 throws, your estimate for π is $\frac{29}{50} = \frac{28}{16\pi}$, hence $\pi = \frac{28\times50}{16\times29} = 3.125$. By increasing the number of throws you will improve your estimate.

There is a good JAVA applet which can be used to extend this task. It builds on the pupils' understanding and creates the concept of a limit for a large number of throws. This applet performs Buffon's experiment using random numbers, and so eliminates any human bias. You will find it at www.angelfire.com/wa/hurben/buff.html

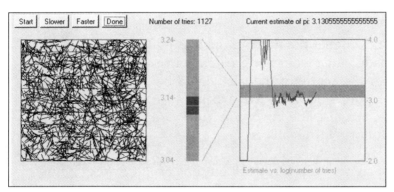

Result of running the JAVA applet at www.angelfire.com/wa/hurben/buff.html

Further references

Beckmann, P. (1971) *A History of π*. New York: St Martin's Press.
Freund, J. (1993) *Introduction to Probability*. New York: Dover.
Gnedenko, B. and Khinchin, A. Ya. (1962) *An Elementary Introduction to the Theory of Probability*, L. F. Boron (trans.), S. F. Mack (ed.). New York: Dover.
Grimmett, G. and Welsh, D. (1986) *Probability: An Introduction*. Oxford: Clarendon Press.

For more on Buffon see:
www. history.mcs.st-and.ac.uk/history/Buffon.html
www.mathforum.org/dr.math
www.angelfire.com/wa/hurben/buff.html

C Cryptology and Ciphers

The world of secret codes has always fascinated young and old alike. There is an air of mystery involved in the world of secret agents trying to discover the enemy's plans before the enemy discovers theirs. In reality most of this work is usually carried out by mathematical boffins in some back room, and not by secret agents sneaking around out there in the real world. This is because the sort of work required to solve these codes is highly logical in its structure.

One famous code-cracking adventure was that of the British code-breakers at Bletchley Park during the Second World War. The Germans used a machine with wheels and electrical rotors called the Enigma machine. Once set up in a certain initial state, the wheels would then automatically turn after each letter was typed. So to decipher the secret code you needed to find out the initial state of the wheels so that you could work backwards through the steps to find the hidden message. Later in this chapter we will look at a simple manual version of the Enigma machine, called a 'polyalphabetic cipher'. It has only two wheels, whereas the Enigma machine has eight wheels.

Alan Turing (1912–1954) was one of the British mathematicians working on this problem during the Second World War. Turing is famous for his work in the development of comput-

The Enigma machine, which was used in the Second World War to produce coded messages

ing. It was in his formative days at Bletchley, when he was working on speeding up the process of decoding messages on the Enigma machine, that he created a very simple computer called a 'bombe'. These bombes were used to test millions of logical assumptions. As Alan Turing said,

since the wheels offer such a large number of permutations of letter selection then we needed to assume a possible setup to start. By running this through the bombe, you could see if it gave any logical contradictions. If a contradiction was found, then by changing the setup you could retest . . . manually the number of setups proved to be impossible to replicate, so the bombe merely takes the place of a human and runs the various start conditions very quickly to find a contradiction . . . This process was still very long, but at least we were only talking hours not weeks!

Experiment time

'Crypto' is from the Greek *kryptos*, meaning hidden or secret. Cryptology is the study of secret systems and methods involved with ciphers. The number of methods which have evolved over the years is directly proportional to the paranoia of the people of the times who wished to hide information.

It starts around 1500BC with the Babylonians. On some of the Babylonian tablets that have been found there are inscriptions for codes. One of these coded messages is a secret recipe for making pottery glaze. There are also references made in Homer's *Iliad* to Greeks using secret codes. King Proetus sends Bellerophon to Lycia with a manuscript containing secret writing. From a military stand, the Spartans were the first to have used cyptography by sending secret codes for troop movements during a battle.

The Polybius method

The Polybius method is a Greek coding system whereby letters are swapped for numbers, as the table below shows.

	1	2	3	4	5
1	A	B	C	D	E
2	F	G	H	IJ	K
3	L	M	N	O	P
4	Q	R	S	T	U
5	V	W	X	Y	Z

So to code the words 'Watch closely and see' you would use column then row to write out the letters in the secret message as follows:

25 11 44 31 32
31 13 43 34 51 13 45
11 33 41
34 51 51

After explaining this system to the class I get them to code messages for the person sitting next to them. This is a good way to introduce the topic. You can then move on to the different types of coding systems introduced below. After each new system allow the class some time to pass messages back and forth. They will find this great fun as the teacher is usually in the opposite position of trying to prevent students passing messages!

The Caesar method

The Caesar method is a cipher which replaces each letter in the alphabet by the letter that is three letters to the right.

Start A B C D E F G H I J K L M N O P Q R S T U V W X Y Z
Code D E F G H I J K L M N O P Q R S T U V W X Y Z A B C

Coding 'Friends, Romans, countrymen' by the Caesar method would give you 'IULHQGV, URPDQV, FRXQWUBPHQ'.

As you can see with both the Polybius method and the Caesar method, there are lots of other possible variations, using letters with numbers or letters with letters. As well as coding a message, I also get the students to create their own secret coding system involving some sort of permutation of the above methods. They can then call it after themselves: 'Hannah's method' or 'Daniel's method'. This personalises their mathematical experience and makes them motivated to find out more.

The polyalphabetic cipher

The polyalphabetic cipher was first used in the fifteenth century, using what is commonly called the cipher disc. This is a manual version of the electronic Enigma machine.

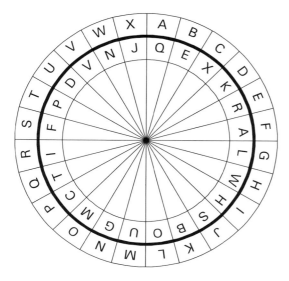

Cipher disc for the polyalphabetic cipher

The disc is divided into 24 equal parts, so that Y and Z remain the same in the code. To add to the difficulty of trying to crack this type of code, the wheel would be turned after each letter.

So by first setting the outer and inner wheel on A, we could then code the first letter. Then turn the inner wheel clockwise two sections and code the second letter. This is then repeated for the whole message. At the end of the message the last letter in the code tells you the position of the outer wheel letter A with the inner wheel. So in the example wheel above, our message ended on Q. There also has to be an agreement between coder and decoder for the number of turns of the wheel before you start.

Another variation on this method was to code another letter at the end of the message, to indicate the number of turns made after each coded letter. For example, if the letter was A this means one turn, if B this means two turns and so on.

With students I tend to start by getting them to make a polyalphabetic cipher. This can be created from two circles, each divided up into 24 parts. The smaller circle is placed in the centre of the larger one and fastened with a paper fastener so that the wheels can rotate. The letters on the smaller central wheel can be placed in any order; the order I use above is the order that was used by Leon Alberti in 1568.

Since this is a more complex coding system than the Polybius and Caesar methods, it's best to start by coding with the students from a stationary wheel, as in the Caesar method. Then code a short sentence by moving the wheel around one space after each letter. The students do not usually find coding a great problem, but problems sometimes occur when it comes to decoding. It is therefore a good idea to give them time to familiarise themselves with the device. Once they have mastered the basics there are several interesting extensions:

1. Code the start position of the wheel for decoding as the first letter in the message.
2. Code two or more letters at the start or end of the message to indicate a periodic change in the turning of the wheel. For example BC would mean that the decoder would need to turn the wheel two spaces then three spaces then two, etc.
3. Code XXX at the end of the coded message to show that everything after that is to do with the wheel.
4. Introduce three or more wheels. This will start to create very complex cryptology.

Encourage the students to extend and develop these methods into their own.

Further references

Hodges, A. (1992) *Alan Turing: The Enigma.* London: Random House.
Kahn, D. (1996) *The Codebreakers: The Story of Secret Writing.* New York: Simon and Schuster.
Stephenson, N. (1999) *Cryptonomicon.* New York: Avon Books.

See also:
the National Cryptologic Museum at www.nsa.gov/museum/
www.enigma-themovie.com
www.codesandciphers.org.uk/enigma

D Dragon Curve

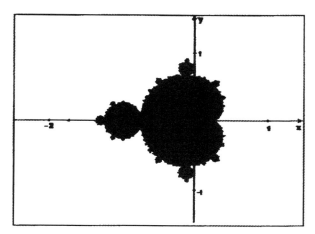

Benoit Mandelbrot (1924–) and the fractal curve named after him, the Mandelbrot set

A fractal is a geometrical figure in which an identical part repeats itself on an ever-decreasing scale. Benoit Mandelbrot is one of the key figures in fractal research. He is the originator of the word 'fractal', which comes from the Latin verb *frangere*, meaning to create irregular fragments. In 1983 he published *The Fractal Geometry of Nature*, which takes a revolutionary view of geometry not seen since the time of Eulid's *Elements* in 300BC. Mandelbrot says, 'Clouds are not spheres, mountains are not cones, the coastline is not a circle, and bark is not smooth nor does lightning travel in a straight line. Generally nature is irregular and fragmented', so we need a way to describe these features which we see around us. Fractals can help us do this. From chemical reactions to ferns and complex turbulent flow of smoke we see fractals in nature's chaos. Fractals have also become the new computer art and can be seen in art galleries and even as posters on students' walls!

It was no coincidence that Mandelbrot worked as a mathematics researcher for IBM, since it is only with the vast power of computers that fractal beauty can truly be seen. For some startling and exciting pictures of fractals, see the websites given in the further references at the end of this chapter.

Experiment time

One fractal curve is called the Dragon Curve. It was discovered by J. E. Heighway in 1978. He called it the Dragon Curve because the meandering line reminded him of a Chinese dragon. Students can see these meanders by first folding paper, then, with the use of a computer, they will be able to generalise the sequence they observe in the paper into a formula for the Dragon Curve.

Fold a long narrow strip of paper in half, as shown here. This gives one left turn.

10 FOLDS. WITH A 90 DEGREE ANGLE

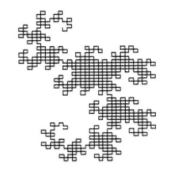

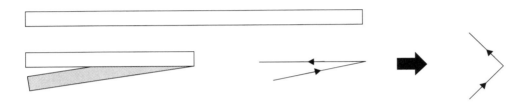

Repeat this, folding in the same direction each time. This gives a left turn, a left turn and a right turn, in that order, as you can see by following the arrows along the lines.

Next, fold again to the three folds. This produces left, left, right, left, left, right, right and left:

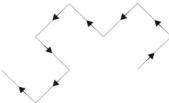

With four folds, and drawing the angles at 100 degrees instead of 90 degrees, we get a curve with 16 sections ($2^4 = 16$):

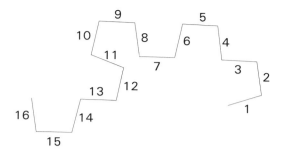

To analyse the folding you need to look to see if the paper turns left or right. Using $d = 1$ to signify a move to the left and $d = -1$ to signify a move to the right, we can obtain the following table.

n	1	2	3	4	5	6	7	8
d	1	1	−1	1	1	−1	−1	1

It is difficult to see a pattern yet. You need to look at the next set of meanders.

n	9	10	11	12	13	14	15	16
d	1	1	−1	−1	1	−1	−1	1

From these a pattern begins to form. Another fold will create a curve with 32 sections and help to confirm these conclusions. Students may find that at this stage it is best to use the computer program called DRAGON on the accompanying CD, as with this number of sections it becomes difficult to check for left and right turns. If you prefer, you can keep folding, but only up to about seven steps ($2^7 = 128$ sections); after this the paper will become very difficult to fold.

From the table we have created it can be seen that factors of 2 play an essential role. We can see that:

$$d(8) = d(4) = d(2) = d(1) = 1$$
$$d(12) = d(6) = d(3) = -1$$
$$d(10) = d(5) = 1$$

With some more work you will find that the general rule is:

$$d(n) = 1 \qquad \text{for } n = 1, 5, 9, 13, \ldots$$
$$d(n) = -1 \qquad \text{for } n = 3, 7, 11, 15, \ldots$$
$$d(n) = d(n/2) \quad \text{for even } n$$

It will take students some time to obtain this generalisation, so it is a good idea to let them experiment with a larger number of folds using DRAGON. They can find d not just for four folds ($p = 4$ in DRAGON, and $n = 16$) as the table above shows, but for 5 ($n = 32$), 6 ($n = 64$) and more. Soon they will be walking with the dragon along its meandering path.

Computer support

There are a number of changes that can be made in the computer program to produce different effects:

- by changing the 4 in line

```
70 H=2^(-P/4)
```

  you can alter the size of the line drawn at each step.

- the line

```
20 WINDOW (-10,-10) - (10,10)
```

  gives the size of the axis on which the Dragon Curve is drawn. At the start it is set with the *x*- and *y*-axes running from –10 to +10. If you wish to increase either axis in either direction you need to change the number on this line.

Extension ideas

Each section of the Dragon Curve has a fixed length and it is the angle that changes. In the program called SPIRAL the opposite is true in that the lengths change and the angle is fixed at 90 degrees.

The program will ask you for the numbers to spiral. If you give, say, 1, 2, 3, it will draw the following pattern. Note that after each number is drawn the following rule is obeyed: TURN: right, up, left, down, repeat.

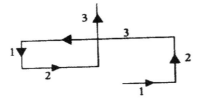
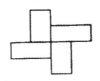

This simple pattern hides a number of secrets to be discovered. I usually start the experimenting by getting the students to draw the first few spirals by hand. Then, when they feel confident reproducing the pattern, move on to the computer. You will find that some students will continue to enjoy drawing the spirals even with the computer program there to help them.

Some patterns are ordered, others are strange. Some examples are shown opposite. Good questions to ask are:

- Which sets of numbers return to their starting point in the spiral?
- Which numbers diverge off the screen?
- Which numbers produce symmetric shapes in the spirals?

Number of spirals = 11
1, 2, 3, 4, 5, 6, 7, 8, 9, 10, 11

Number of spirals = 13
1, 2, 5, 4, 0, 6, 3, 5, 4, 2, 6, 7, 2

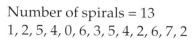

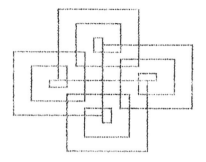

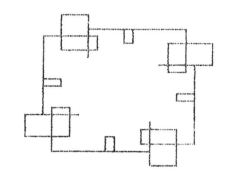

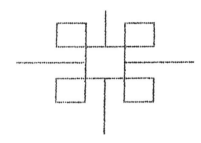

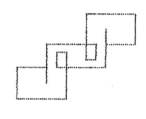

Computer support

- After telling the computer the number of numbers to spiral, enter each one by pressing return.
- With the line

```
15 WINDOW (-500, -500)-(500, 500)
```

the axes are set for values from −500 to +500. To see some of the diverging spirals you may want to increase this.

- Modern day computers are very fast, so you will find that the line

```
125 FOR E = 1 TO 10000: NEXT E
```

and others like it in the code are there to slow things down so you can see what is happening. If you want to slow it down further, increase the 10 000 to 20 000 or more.

Further references

Barnsley, M. F. (1993) *Fractals Everywhere*. London: Academic Press Professional.

Becker, K.-H. and Dorfler, M. (1989) *Dynamical Systems and Fractals*, I. Stewart (trans.). Cambridge: Cambridge University Press.

Devaney, R. L. (1990) *Chaos, Fractals and Dynamics: Computer Experiments in Mathematics*. Menlo Park, CA: Addison Wesley.

Gleick, J. (1987) *Chaos: Making a New Science*. New York: Viking Penguin.

The following websites may also be of interest:
www.fractalus.com/
www.softlab.ntua.gr/mandel
www.cln.org/themes/fractals.html

E Euler and Polyhedra

Two islands in a river are connected to the banks by seven bridges, as shown. Can you cross all the bridges in one journey, not going back over the same bridge more than once?

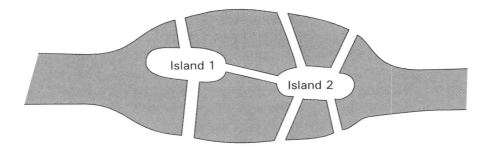

Island 1

Island 2

This is called the Konigsberg bridge problem. Euler created a new discipline in mathematics in order to prove that this journey is not possible: topology. Euler's work in mathematics is so vast that you would have trouble learning it all in a lifetime. He is the most prolific writer in mathematics who has ever lived. He worked in most of the prominent areas of mathematics known in the eighteenth century and instigated a number of new areas of mathematical research which he discovered himself.

Euler left his name indelibly marked in the history of mathematics with his discovery of the number that we now call Euler's number, $e = 2.718\,281\,828\,459\,045\ldots$

It is a number like π, and in just the same strange way it appears all over the place in mathematics, in theories of atoms, planets, water flow and finance, to name a few. It is called a universal constant. When I talk about

Swiss mathematicin Leonhard Euler (1707–1783)

it I always tell my students that 'it is the natural base to count in. This is why we call its inverse function the natural logarithm. We count in tens because we have ten fingers, but somewhere out in space there will be some little green men counting in 2.71s...'

You can work out more digits for e using the following Taylor series (see Chapter T):

$$e^x = 1 + x + \frac{x^2}{2!} + \frac{x^3}{3!} + \frac{x^4}{4!} + \ldots$$

The exclamation marks stand for factorials. These are defined as follows:

$1! = 1$ $2! = 1 \times 2$ $3! = 1 \times 2 \times 3$ $4! = 1 \times 2 \times 3 \times 4$, and so on.

In 1737 Euler proved that e is irrational, that is, it cannot be written as a fraction. Here is his proof.

Using the above series with $x = 1$ gives

$$e = 1 + \frac{1}{1!} + \frac{1}{2!} + \frac{1}{3!} + \ldots$$

Assume that e can be written as a fraction, say $e = \frac{p}{q}$, where p and q are integers with no common factors. Let $e = a + b$, where

$$a = 1 + \frac{1}{1!} + \frac{1}{2!} + \frac{1}{3!} + \ldots \frac{1}{q!} \quad \text{and} \quad b = \frac{1}{(q+1)!} + \frac{1}{(q+2)!} + \frac{1}{(q+3)!} + \ldots$$

Multiplying both sides of the equation $e = a + b$ by $q!$ gives

$$eq! = aq! + bq!$$

Now, since $aq!$ is an integer and $eq!$ is an integer, it follows that $bq!$ is the difference of two integers, which is another integer. However,

$$bq! = \frac{1}{(q+1)} + \frac{1}{(q+1)(q+2)} + \frac{1}{(q+1)(q+2)(q+3)} + \ldots \quad < \quad \frac{1}{2} + \frac{1}{4} + \frac{1}{8} + \ldots \quad < \quad 1$$

implying that $bq! < 1$. But we know that $bq!$ is an integer, so we have a contradiction. Our initial hypothesis that e can be written as a fraction must be wrong. Therefore e is irrational.

Konigsberg is now part of Russia, and was renamed Kaliningrad after President Mikhail Kalinin, but in Euler's day it was the capital of the German state of East Prussia. As you stand on one of Konigsberg's bridges you see the city's Teutonic legacy in its architecture. It is said that Euler loved his Sunday afternoon strolls over these bridges. You can imagine him admiring the impressive buildings. His gaze may have been drawn to the masonry and ironwork of these buildings, which feature many polyhedrons. Maybe this was what prompted his famous formula relating edges, vertices and faces of polyhedrons:

$$V + F = E + 2$$

where V is the number of vertices (corners), F is the number of faces and E is the number of edges. With a cube, for example,

$V = 8$
$F = 6$
$E = 12$

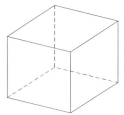

Applying Euler's formula,

$8 + 6 = 12 + 2$

Worksheet for construction of solids

Tetrahedron

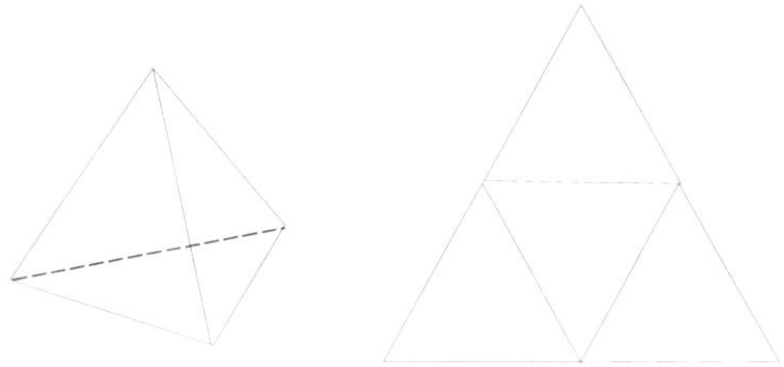

Cube

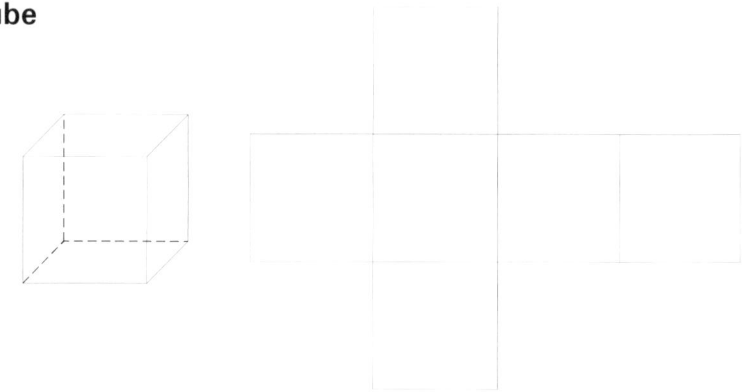

Octahedron

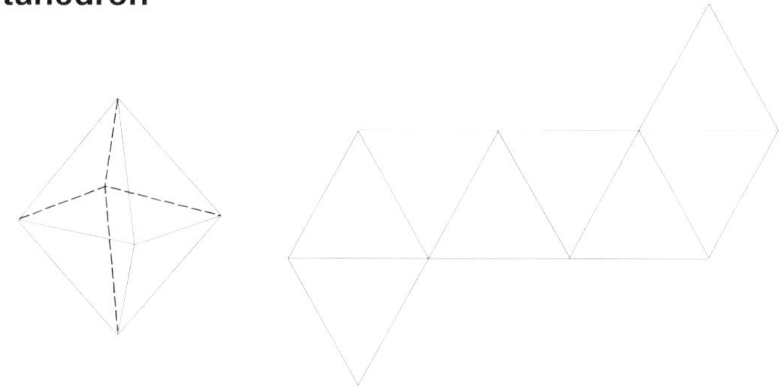

Dodecahedron

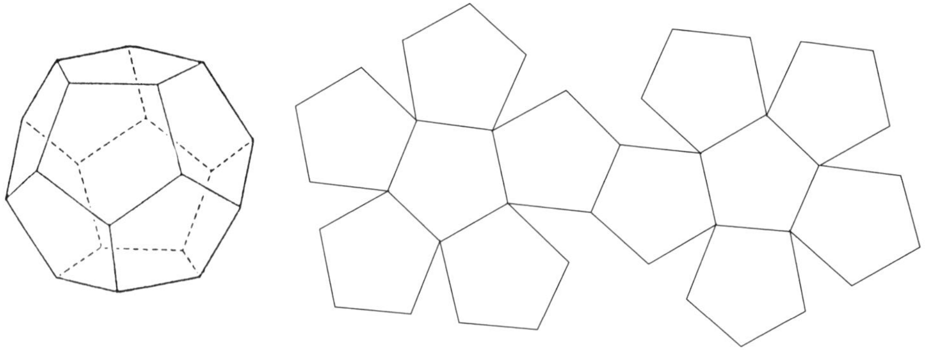

Icosahedron

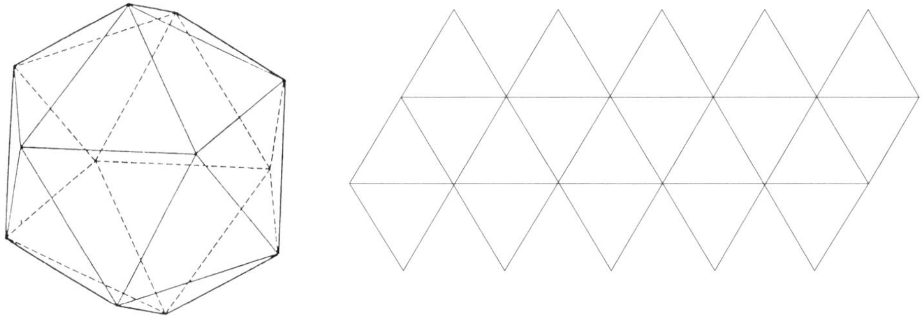

Experiment time

Using the worksheet provided, get the students to construct some of these polyhedra. All students gain from handling the three-dimensional models and the better students will enjoy the challenge of creating some of the harder models. It is best to construct these using card, joining the edges with tape or glued tabs. A number of educational stockists supply these types of models, but the time taken to construct these three-dimensional shapes is time well spent and will benefit the students greatly in the future.

Ask the students to count vertices, faces and edges, then check to see if these satisfy Euler's formula. While they are doing this ask them to look for simple counting techniques, such as faces are joined at edges and edges are joined at vertices. This will help them to check that they get the correct answers.

Regular polyhedron	Number of vertices	Number of faces	Number of edges
Tetrahedron	4	4	6
Hexahedron (cube)	8	6	12
Octahedron	6	8	12
Dodecahedron	20	12	30
Icosahedron	12	20	30
n-Prism	$n + 2$	$2n$	$3n$
n-Pyramid	$n + 1$	$n + 1$	$2n$

The final two generalisations for specific cases create useful extensions. The 4-Prism is the cube and the 3-Pyramid is the tetrahedron.

Extension ideas

1. An interesting question involves colouring the faces. If the faces of each solid are painted, each entirely with a single colour, what is the least number of colours needed to paint each solid such that no two adjacent faces have the same colour? There are a number of interesting patterns that can be found.
2. If you cut off the corners of the cube in the following stages you get this interesting sequence:

cube	6 square faces
truncated cube	6 octagonal and 8 triangular faces
cuboctahedron	6 square and 8 triangular faces
truncated octahedron	6 square and 8 hexagonal faces
octahedron	8 triangular faces

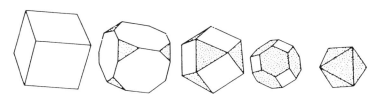

Asking students to check Euler's formula for these polyhedra and/or construct a complete set of these models is a good extension task for the more able.

Further references

Cundy, H. Martyn and Rolett, A. P. (1981) *Mathematical Models*, 3rd edn. Norfolk: Tarquin Publications (2nd edn, 1961, Oxford: Clarendon Press).

Hilton, P. and Pedersen, J. (1994) *Build Your Own Polyhedra*. Menlo Park, CA: Addison Wesley.

Jenkins, G., Bear, M. and Bear, M. (1999) *Paper Polyhedra in Colour*. Norfolk: Tarquin Publications.

Simon, L. Arnstein, B. and Gurkewitz, R. (1989) *Modular Origami Polyhedra*. New York: Dover Publications.

For more information about Euler, see:
www-history.mcs.st-and.ac.uk/history/Mathematicians/Euler

F Feigenbaum Number

The Feigenbaum number $\delta = 4.669\,201\,609\,102\,990\,9\ldots$ was discovered by Mitchell Feigenbaum in 1978. It is a universal constant just like e and π (see Chapters E and P). Because of its recent discovery it is not as well known as these other constants, but in years to come it may well feature on your calculator just as e and π do now.

The American mathematician Mitchell Feigenbaum (1944–)

The flow behind an aeroplane wing is called the Karman vortex street. This name comes from the fact that the swirling vortices form a row, or street, as they peel off the wing. This fact was first noticed in 1962 by Theodor von Karman, a Hungarian fluid dynamicist. You can see these vortices when you watch an aeroplane take off from the runway. As the speed of the aeroplane increases the row of vortices lose their ordered appearance and become turbulent. There is little understanding of the behaviour of this turbulence, yet as you can imagine it is very important when you are designing aeroplanes.

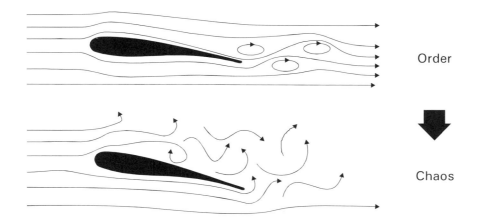

Order

Chaos

Mitchell Feigenbaum was working on turbulence at Los Alamos National Laboratory. He was interested in the initial stage of turbulence, as order changes into chaos. This can be seen in a number of everyday things apart from aeroplanes, such as a rising column of smoke from a candle, which breaks into wild swirls as the order is lost. Feigenbaum started to think about problems such as these and soon realised that his education had taught him very little. He had to go back to a very simple equation and try to understand how turbulence affected it before he could go on to some of the bigger problems in turbulent flow.

The equation he picked was one that models the seasonal population of moths or fish. After repeated calculation using this equation the answer will become constant, and at this point the biological balance between population and environment has been reached. Feigenbaum started calculating, and for some initial conditions this single answer was reached. For other sets of initial conditions he would get two, four, eight or even sixteen answers. This doubling in the number of solutions to an equation is called periodic doubling. In terms of biology, periodic doubling indicates that the seasonal population varies from year to year in a periodic manner. Feigenbaum started to look for a case in which there were so many answers that the doubling would never stop. Due to the slowness of computers in 1978, Fiegenbaum had spare time while the computer was doing the next calculation. He used this time to experiment with the answers he had already found and would try to guess the next answer. After a few months he became very good at calculating the correct answer. He found some unexpected regularity hidden in the chaotic mess: a pattern in turbulence.

With such an important discovery he had to be sure. He increased his working day to 22 hours, taking only short breaks for food and drink. His friends said that he was shaking with adrenaline, unable to talk about anything but numbers. In the end, after two months of this, his doctor said he must stop or die. Fiegenbaum stopped and took a long vacation, for by then he knew that he had found a number that was very special.

Experiment time

This iterative equation is the one that Feigenbaum initially worked on:

$$x_{n+1} = px_n(1-x_n) \qquad \text{where } x \in [0,1] \text{ and } p \in [0,4]$$

When your students start working on this equation, they will find it useful to perform some calculations and draw some graphs by hand.

Start with $p = 2$ and the first value $x_1 = 0.1$. Putting these values into the iterative equation above we get:

$$x_2 = 2x_1(1-x_1)$$
$$= 2 \times 0.1 \times (1-0.1) = 0.18$$

Putting this value of x_2 back into the equation we get:

$$x_3 = 2x_2(1-x_2)$$
$$= 2 \times 0.18 \times (1-0.18) = 0.2952$$

If you keep repeating this process the next five answers are 0.41611392, 0.485926251, 0.499603859, 0.499999686 and 0.5. They converge to a fixed value, so the equation is in its ordered state. The students should then draw the graphs of $y = x$ and $y = 2x(1-x)$ on one set of axes.

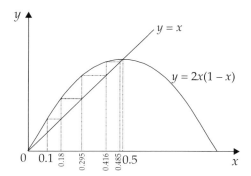

From these it is clear that the values tend to a solution point. After trying a few other cases, such as $p = 1.5$ and $p = 2.5$, you are ready to introduce the students to computer support. The program called FEIGN works out the numbers in the iterative method and the one called FEIGGRAPH draws the graph showing the path of the iteration.

I tell the students that the equation simulates the seasonal population of moths or fish. The p represents the rate of population growth and $(1 - x)$ and x are opposites, such that when one increases the other falls, so keeping the growth within bounds. The magnitude of the population in generation $n + 1$ is x_{n+1}, and is related to the magnitude of the population in the preceding generation n, which is x_n. I also tell them that to keep the graph in the interval $[0,1]$, p must be in the interval $[0,4]$.

Allow the students to experiment with the equation to get a feel for how the different parameters interact. As they discover what could happen you'll hear comments like:

- Growth $p = \frac{1}{2}$ 'Oh no! They all die'
- Growth $p = 5$ 'They have eaten all the food'
- Growth $p = 1$ 'No growth'
- Growth $p = 4$ 'What's this mess?'

You will find that with help the students will try to explain what is going on for the different values of p. When $p = 4$ it is completely turbulent and we have chaos. At first this disordered state will confuse the students, so you will need to teach them a little more about how the equations work. You will find the following information useful:

- x needs to remain in the interval $[0,1]$ because for $x > 1$ the iterations diverge, so the population becomes extinct.
- $px(1 - x)$ has a maximum value of $\frac{p}{4}$, so p must be less than 4.
- If $p < 1$ all trajectories are attracted to $x = 0$, so for $p < 1$ the population becomes extinct.
- A solution (or fixed point or equilibrium value) for the equation is reached when $x_{n+1} = x_n = x$. This gives $x = 0$ (trivial solution) and $x = 1 - \frac{1}{p}$ (zero population growth).
- The stability of the equilibrium point depends on the gradient of $px(1 - x)$. This is stable so long as x lies between -1 and $+1$.
- The slope of $px(1 - x)$ is $(2 - p)$ at the equilibrium point. So the equation is stable for all trajectories starting in the interval $1 < p < 3$.
- For p greater than 3 things get interesting and periodic doubling starts to occur. For example, when $p = 3.2$ the solutions are 0.513 and 0.7995, period two. When $p = 3.5$ the solutions are 0.5, 0.87, 0.38 and 0.82, period four. This is the sort of doubling that Feigenbaum discovered.
- For $3.835 < p < 3.855$ you get an interesting set of solutions with period three!

The following table gives the p value for the start of these doubles.

p	Period	Increase in p	Ratio of increases
3.449499	4	0.449499	
3.544090	8	0.094591	4.75
3.564407	16	0.020313	4.66
3.568759	32	0.004352	4.66
3.569692	64	0.000933	4.67
3.569891	124	0.000199	4.7
3.569934	248	0.000043	4.6

Feigenbaum worked on these increases in the ratio of p values and found his special number. You may think that this is an amazing result, yet this was only the start for him. His two-month quest took him on the trail of hundreds of different equations, some very different from this one, and yet he always found that the same number occurred. In 1979 Oscar Lanford proved that the Feigenbaum number was a true universal constant for all equations. This proof made Feigenbaum one of the greatest mathematicians that the world will ever see.

Extension ideas

Feigenbaum worked on many other equations to check the validity of his number. A good extension for students is to do the same. Here are a few good equations to try, but remember that his number is universally true so you could use any equation.

1. $x_{n+1} = px_n^2(1-x_n)$ in the region $4 \le p \le 7$

2. $x_{n+1} = px_n(1-x_n^2)$ and other powers of x_n

3. $x_{n+1} = p\sin(x_n)\cos(x_n)$ where x is measured in radians ($180° = \pi$ radians)

4. square and cube root functions

Computer support

- For example, to change FEIGN to use the first equation in the extension ideas, change the line

      70 Y=P*X*(1-X)

  to   `70 Y=P*X*X*(1-X)`

  You will be able to find solutions to this equation.

- To get the graph for the first equation in the extension ideas you have to change two lines in FEIGGRAPH:

      70   Y=P*X*(1-X)   to   70   Y=P*X*X*(1-X)
  and 115 Y=P*GX*(1-GX)   to 115 Y=P*GX*GX*(1-GX)

Further references

Baker, G. L. and Gollub, J. P. (1996) *Chaotic Dynamics*. Cambridge: Cambridge University Press.

Becker, K.-H. and Dorfler, M. (1989) *Dynamical Systems and Fractals*, I. Stewart (trans.). Cambridge: Cambridge University Press.

Cvitanovi, P. (1989) *Universality in Chaos*. New York: Adam Hilger.

Gleick, J. (1987) *Chaos: Making a New Science*. New York: Viking Penguin.

See also:
www.library.thinkquest.org/

G Gambling, Probability and Abraham de Moivre

Abraham de Moivre is famous for his formula

$$(\cos x + i \sin x)^n = \cos (nx) + i \sin(nx)$$

which had profound effects on the uses of trigonometry in mathematics. This formula is also linked to one of the most beautiful formulas in mathematics, $e^{\pi i} + 1 = 0$, which links the five most important constants in mathematics. These are $0, 1, e = 2.718281\ldots$ (see chapter E), $\pi = 3.141592\ldots$ (see Chapter P) and $i = \sqrt{-1}$. Why are these five seemingly unrelated fundamental numbers linked in one equation? Professor Feynman, the Nobel prize-winning physicist, states that this is one of the most remarkable formulas known to man; he says 'it is a jewel'.

De Moivre is also famous for predicting the day on which he would die. In later life he noticed that he was sleeping an extra 15 minutes longer each night. By calculating the number of 15-minute intervals in 24 hours, he calculated that on a certain day in the future that he would sleep forever. He was right! If I tell you that he died on 27 November 1754 and that he always used to sleep for eight hours before he noticed this increase, you'll be able to work out when this thought came to him.

De Moivre's book, *The Doctrine of Chances*, published in 1718, changed the way we view probability. In its time the book was a great success, selling to a wide range of readers. Some of the people who bought his book were academics, as De Moivre was well known in English academic circles having been elected as a Fellow of the Royal Society of Mathematics. He was also a good friend of Sir Isaac Newton (see Chapter N), and so met some of the greatest mathematicians of the time through this friendship. Yet his book was also very popular with gamblers, for it was from them that De Moivre's background research in the book had been collected. In the eighteenth century, coffee houses were the same as casinos are now. De Moivre spent many an hour sitting in these coffee houses working on his

French mathematician Abraham de Moivre (1667–1754)

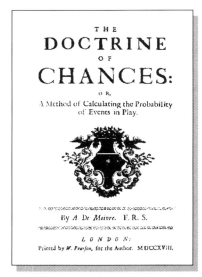

The title page of de Moivre's famous book, published in 1718

theory of probability. In the corner of the coffee houses would be tables where one could sit and drink coffee. In the rest of the smoke-filled room people would be playing various games of chance, many of which would involve dice. De Moivre would sit drinking coffee and offer advice to gamblers on the correct strategy to use to win these games. He would charge a small fee for this advice, but mainly he was interested in the results of the experiments that the gamblers were about to perform for him. The experimental results that he collected in these coffee houses would eventually become the laws of probability that we know today. Once his book was published he became famous, and gamblers came from miles away to take mathematics lessons with him. Can you imagine the scene? Hundreds of students queuing up to take maths classes!

Experiment time

With experimental probability you are looking to see what happens as the number of trials tends to a large number. This is a difficult concept for most people to imagine, as in everyday life we will only register a few trials and then try to make some judgement on the basis of these. Yet this may not tell you the whole truth, as the first few trials may be affected by something and so give a biased result.

Coins

With a class you have the perfect environment to do large-scale trials. So let's ask a question. When you throw two coins, what is the chance that you get two heads? To answer this question divide the students into pairs, giving each pair two coins. Get them to complete a table as shown below, as they perform the 20 trials.

Trials	1	2	3	4	5	6	7	8	9	10	11	12	...
Two heads	•				•					•	•		
Not two heads		•	•	•		•	•	•	•				•	...
Probability of throwing two heads	$\frac{1}{1}$	$\frac{1}{2}$	$\frac{1}{3}$	$\frac{1}{4}$	$\frac{2}{5}$	$\frac{2}{6}$	$\frac{2}{7}$	$\frac{2}{8}$	$\frac{2}{9}$	$\frac{3}{10}$	$\frac{4}{11}$	$\frac{4}{12}$	...
Percentage success	1	0.5	0.33	0.25	0.4	0.33	0.28	0.25	0.22	0.3	...		

They can also plot this data on a graph, like this:

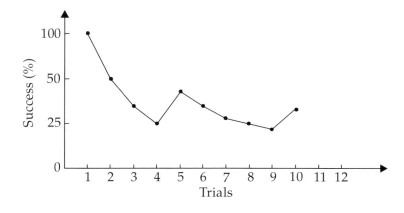

31

When you collect the results from all the pairs, there will be a clear pattern showing all the results tending towards 25% or a probability of $\frac{1}{4}$. This shows that over a number of trials the cumulative fractions will tend to the true probability of getting two heads.

Why does the experiment give us this value?

The expansion of $(T + H)^2$ gives all the possible combinations of results when tossing two coins. Thus, from $(T + H)^2 = TT + 2TH + HH$, we know that the result could be two tails, a tail and a head (in two possible ways) and two heads. This method also allows you to develop into the probability of getting three, four or five heads when tossing three, four or five coins, using other expansions:

$(T + H)^3 = TTT + 3TTH + 3THH + HHH$
$(T + H)^4 = TTTT + 4TTTH + 6TTHH + 4THHH + HHHH$
$(T + H)^5 = TTTTT + 5TTTTH + 10\,TTTHH + 10\,TTHHH + 5THHHH + HHHHH$

The coefficients in these expansions come from Pascal's triangle (see Chapter V), or by multiplying out the above brackets.

Let's ask another question. What is the chance of throwing two heads with only four coins?

From the expansion for $(T + H)^4$ above, which is the expansion we would use for four coins, we can see that the coefficient for the combination with two heads is 6. The number of possible combinations when tossing four coins is the sum of the coefficients, $1 + 4 + 6 + 4 + 1 = 16$. So the probability of throwing two heads with four coins is $\frac{6}{16}$. If they were asked to gamble in a game which asked them to throw exactly two heads, I think you would find that most students would think the chance to be $\frac{1}{2}$, and that it was therefore a fair game, but in fact they would be likely to lose.

If the rules of the game were receive £3 if you win (toss two heads) and pay out £2 if you lose, should you play? Well, let's look to see what happens on average.

$$\text{win} = 3 \times \tfrac{3}{8} = \tfrac{9}{8}$$
$$\text{lose} = 2 \times \tfrac{5}{8} = \tfrac{10}{8}$$

So adding up your winnings and subtracting your losses, on average in a game you would lose $\frac{9}{8} - \frac{10}{8} = -\frac{1}{8} = -0.125$. This may not seem much, but when you multiply this up to, say, 100 games, you would lose, on average, £12.50. A gambler would only want to play a game which gave a greater expected probability for winning, unlike this one which comes out with negative average return.

Dice

Lets move on to dice games. The first reference to dice being used in games of chance was in Egypt in 3000BC. Since then they have played an important role in reproducing random events and providing chance. In the seventeenth century, Chevalier de Mere, a French aristocrat and notorious gambler, asked the mathematicians of the time to help him win at a game called *non double*. It was a game of the time whereby you had to throw a double 6 in 24 throws of two dice for an even money return. If students were asked to take a chance and play this game they may say yes. They would know that the probability of throwing a double 6 with one roll of two dice is $\frac{1}{36}$. So in 24 rolls, would the chance be $\frac{24}{36}$? By this logic, if we rolled the dice 37 times the chance would be $\frac{37}{36}$, and you cannot have a probability greater than 1, so something is clearly wrong. The correct way to think of the problem is by finding the probability of *not* getting a double 6. This must be $1 - \frac{1}{36} = \frac{35}{36}$. The probability of not getting a double 6 in 24 rolls is $\frac{35}{36}$ multiplied by itself 24 times, or $\left(\frac{35}{36}\right)^{24}$. Subtracting this from 1 (certainty) gives the chance of getting at least one double 6 in 24 rolls, as $1 - \left(\frac{35}{36}\right)^{24} = 0.4914\ldots$. This is a little under $\frac{1}{2}$, so the gambler has a little less than evens chance of winning. As you saw from before, this would not a be game to play because in the long run you would lose on average.

Some students will be unsure of the answer to these questions, so it is a good experiment to perform with the class. Split the class as with the first experiment. Get each pair to throw the dice 24 times and see how many pairs get two 6s. Then create a table using the pairs' results to find the value of the probability. This class result will probably come out to 0.5, and so will create some interesting discussion about whether to play the game or not.

Extension ideas

1. Other classic probability questions:
- **Chevalier de Mere:** Find the probability of at least one 6 in four tosses of a fair dice.
- **Galileo and the Duke of Tuscany:** Compare the probability of a total of 9 with the probability of a total of 10 when three dice are tossed.
- **Pepys to Newton:** Compare the probability of at least one 6 when six dice are tossed with the probability of at least two 6s, when 12 dice are tossed.
2. In 1730, James Stirling published an approximate formula to calculate the probability of an equal number of heads and tails when you throw any even number of coins. It is given by $1/\sqrt{n\pi}$ with n equal to the number of heads or tails. For example, with four coins (2H and 2T), $n = 2$ so the probability is $1/\sqrt{2\pi}$, which as you can see is close to our answer of 0.375. This formula also tells us that as the number of coin tosses increases, the chance of getting an equal number of heads and tails decreases. Yet we know the number of heads tends to around 0.5. It just shows, there is no such thing as certainty!
3. Using real-life games, such as football results, can create interesting probability lessons:
- Look at the team's previous form. Can we predict future wins?
- Look at the odds given by bookmakers and see how these relate to the team's performance.
- What is the most important factor in future wins?
- Carry out a football project and update the probabilities weekly for each team.

Further references

David, F. N. (1962) *Games, Gods and Gambling*. London: Griffin.

Epstein, R. A. (1977) *The Theory of Gambling and Statistical Logic*. London and New York: Academic Press.

Goldberg, S. (1987) *Probability: An Introduction*. New York: Dover

Westergaard, H. (1932) *Contributions to the History of Statistics*. London: King.

See also:

www.cut-the-knot.com/probability.html

http://mathforum.org/library/topics/

www.mathcs.carleton.edu/probweb/probweb.html

H Hanoi Towers

Édouard Lucas taught mathematics in Paris at Lycée Charlemagne in the late nineteenth century. In 1883 he published a book of recreational mathematics which has since become a four-volume classic. The original book was published under the name M. Claus, which is an anagram of his name. His book gives the first documented version of the Tower of Hanoi puzzle, introduced by an interesting story. The story claims that the tower is a device used by monks waiting for the end of the world. In Lucas's book, the Tower of Hanoi puzzle is called the Tower of Brahma, and the whole tale is set in a Indian temple in the city of Benares.

French mathematician
Édouard Lucas (1842–1891)

In the great temple at Benares beneath the dome which marks the centre of the world, rests a brass plate in which are fixed three diamond needles, each a cubit high and as thick as the body of a bee. On one of these needles, at the creation, God placed sixty four discs of pure gold, the largest disc resting on the brass plate and the others getting smaller and smaller up to the top one. This is the Tower of Brahma. Day and night unceasingly, the priests transfer the discs from one diamond needle to another, according to the fixed and immutable laws of Brahma, which require that the priest on duty must not move more than one disc at a time and that he must place this disc on a needle so that there is no smaller disc below it. When the sixty-four discs shall have been thus transferred from the needle on which, at the creation, God placed them, to one of the other needles, tower, temple, and Brahmans alike will crumble into dust, and with a thunderclap, the world will vanish.

Experiment time

The object of the Tower of Hanoi game is to transfer all the discs to one of the other pegs under the following conditions:

1. Move only one disc at a time.
2. No disc may be placed on top of one smaller than itself.
3. Use the fewest possible moves.

After explaining the rules of the game to the students they should be allowed to try to complete the task in the smallest number of moves. You can use three discs or coins to play

34

Hanoi Towers game with three discs　　　Hanoi Towers game with three coins

this game. The discs can be made from card or you can use three different sized coins. With three objects only seven moves are required.

Once the students have completed the puzzle with three objects, they can move on to four objects. For four objects, under the same rules, it takes 15 moves to complete the puzzle, and for five objects 31 moves are required. The students will start to see a pattern forming. In general, for n objects, $2^n - 1$ moves are required.

The explanation of this formula can be seen if we look at the number of moves required for four objects.

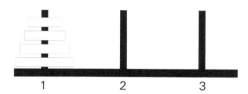

Let a_4 be the number of moves needed to solve the four-object problem. First move three discs on to needle 2. This is a three-object problem, so lets call it a_3. We won't worry about how to move these three discs onto needle 2 at present. We will just assume that it is possible in the least number of moves.

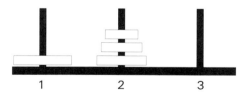

Then move the largest ring from needle 1 to needle 3. This is one move.

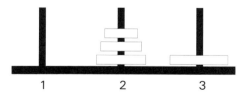

Now move the three rings from needle 2 to needle 3. Don't worry about how this is done. Think of it as a three-object problem, so the number of moves required for this stage is a_3.

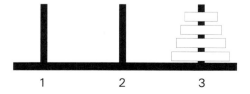

So we have solved the four-object problem if we know how to solve the three-object problem. In mathematical terms, following the above steps can be written as

$$a_4 = a_3 + 1 + a_3$$

That is,
$$a_4 = 2a_3 + 1$$

To solve the n-object problem we can generalise this rule to give

$$a_n = 2a_{n-1} + 1$$

By substituting $a_n = 2^n - 1$ into our generalised rule, it can be shown to be the solution.

What about the initial problem? How many moves would it take for 64 discs? Using the above formula gives the number of moves as

$$2^{64} - 1 = 18\ 446\ 744\ 073\ 709\ 551\ 615$$

It's a good idea to ask the students to estimate how long it would take the monks to complete the task for 64 discs. Before they start to calculate they will need to agree on the time it takes to move one disc. You will find that the world seems safe from the destruction talked about in the story!

Extension ideas

One of the reasons why Édouard Lucas created this puzzle was his great interest in numbers of the form $2^n - 1$, especially when n is a prime number (see Chapter M). In 1876 Lucas proved that the number $2^{127} - 1$ is prime. In all its glory the number is

$$2^{127} - 1 = 170\ 141\ 183\ 460\ 469\ 231\ 731\ 687\ 303\ 715\ 884\ 105\ 727$$

This number remains the largest prime number to be discovered without the use of a computer.

This and other primes which can be written in this form are called Mersenne primes. Martin Mersenne was a French cleric who did a large amount of the early work on such numbers in the seventeenth century. Students are able to check the first few of these types of numbers to see if they are primes, but they very quickly go beyond mental arithmetic or even the use of a calculator. Here are the first few:

$$2^2 - 1 = 3$$
$$2^3 - 1 = 7$$
$$2^5 - 1 = 31$$
$$2^7 - 1 = 127$$
$$2^{13} - 1 = 8191$$
$$2^{17} - 1 = 131\ 071$$

The other values of n for which the equation $2^n - 1$ gives a prime number are 19, 31, 61, 89, 107, 127, 521, 607, 1279, 2203, 2281, 3217, 4253, 4423, 9689, 9941, 11 213, 19 937, 21 701, 23 209, 44 497, 86 243, 110 503, 132 049, 216 091, 756 839, 859 433, 1 257 787, 1 398 269, 2 976 221 and 3 021 377. The most recent Mersenne prime discovered has an n value of 3 021 377. This was proved to be prime by R. Clarkson from California University in 1998. It is a 909 526-digit number. It is still unknown, not yet proved, whether there are an infinite number of Mersenne primes. Mathematicians are still working on this problem and have been doing so since the first one was discovered some 2400 years ago. Some problems take a long time to solve!

Further references

Bezuska, S. *et al.* (1980) *Perfect Numbers*. Boston, MA: Boston College Mathematics Institute.

Carroll, L. (1958) *Mathematical Recreations of Lewis Carroll*. New York: Dover Publications.

Gardiner, M. (1996) *The Universe in a Handkerchief : Lewis Carroll's Mathematical Recreations, Games, Puzzles, and Word Plays*. New York: Copernicus.

Lucas, É. (1882–94) *Récréations Mathématiques*, four volumes. Paris: Gauthier-Villars, Paris (reprinted by Blanchard, Paris in 1959).

To control a robot performing the Towers of Hanoi puzzle, see www.fh-konstanz.de/studium/ze/cim/projekte/webcam/

See also:
www.geocities.com/jiprolog/HanoiApp

The following websites give computer games for Towers of Hanoi:
http://privat.schlund.de/R/RoschmannFriedrich/frame.htm
www.aspecialplace.net/Games/
www.dcs.napier.ac.uk/a.cumming/hanoi/

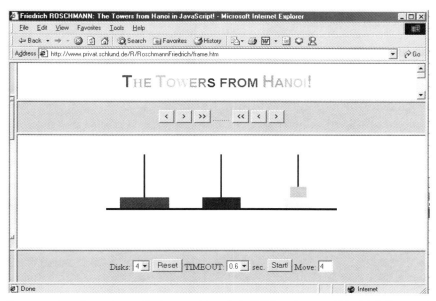

Screen shot from http://privat.schlund.de/R/RoschmannFriedrich/frame.htm showing the puzzle in progress

▐ Integers and Lagrange

When I talk to my students about the great mathematicians of the past, one difficulty that always appears is the idea of greatness. They believe that I, as their teacher, know all the maths there is to know, so when I tell them that compared with Joseph-Louis Lagrange my mathematical ability is the same as that of a 3-year-old who can just about count to ten, and has little understanding about what it means to count, let alone any idea of place value, they look slightly puzzled. I tell them that if Lagrange had been an athlete he would have run the 100 m in 3 seconds flat. 'No one can do that,' they reply. 'Yes, that's what I mean. You think that it is impossible, but when Lagrange put his ideas down on paper the whole of the mathematics community of the time just said "We did not think it was possible".'

The great French mathematician Joseph-Louis Lagrange (1736–1813)

The great mathematicians are great for this reason. They stand alone in their time, understanding more than anyone had ever thought was possible. Lagrange was such a man. By the age of 19 he was already a professor of mathematics for his ideas on how objects always moved on the path of least energy. Lagrange created this new theory working alone. The same theory was used recently to prove that light does not travel in a straight line, but somehow searches out the path that takes the shortest time. This is why you see what seems like water on the road on a hot day. This mirage is created by light travelling from the sun to your eye via the hot road. The route is just as quick as the direct one to your eye, since the hot air has made some of the particles move up off the road, leaving a route with fewer obstacles for the light to bump into.

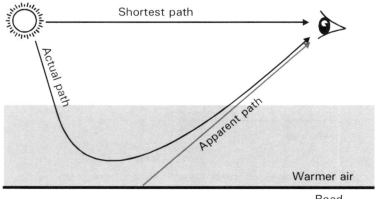

Lagrange's life-work covered topics such as sound, fluids, orbits of the planets and comets, probability and, of course, numbers. In this chapter I will concentrate on his great insight in the area of numbers.

In 1771 Lagrange proved a famous result in number theory all about primes (see Chapter M). Before I explain this result I need to tell you a little about arithmetic sequences. An arithmetic sequence is a pattern of numbers such as 3, 5, 7, 9, 11, . . . or 23, 30, 37, 44, . . ., where the difference between successive numbers in the pattern is the same: 2 and 7 in these examples, respectively. An arithmetic sequence always has a regular pattern between the consecutive numbers.

Lagrange proved that in an arithmetic sequence of three primes, where none of the numbers is 3, the difference is some multiple of 6. For example, the arithemetic sequences 7, 13, 19 and 17, 29, 41 have differences of 6 and 12, respectively.

This is interesting, but why is he famous for this? Well, Lagrange went on to look at other groups of primes. In an arithmetic sequence of five primes, where none of the numbers is 5, the difference is a multiple of 30. One example of such a sequence is 571, 601, 631, 661, 691. Note that 30 can be written as $2 \times 3 \times 5$, that is, the produce of all the primes less than or equal to 5.

We are starting to see a pattern. The next prime is 7, and if you take an arithmetic sequence of 7 prime numbers you will find that the difference is divisible by a multiple of 210, which is a product of all the primes up to 7. With 11 primes the difference is a multiple of $2 \times 3 \times 5 \times 7 \times 11 = 462$, and so on. This means that we have a pattern for a large number of primes. This is an amazing result. Before Lagrange discovered this pattern, it was thought by the mathematical community that there was no pattern in prime numbers.

A proof of the case for three primes

Assume that the difference between the numbers is not divisible by 3. The difference can therefore be written $3a + b$, where a and b are integers and $0 < b < 3$. Writing the three numbers as multiples of 3 and remainders, they are: $3c + r$, $3(a + c) + r + b$ and $3(2a + c) + r + 2b$. So, given that $0 < b < 3$, the remainders when the numbers in the sequence are divided by 3 are all different. But since each has a different remainder, one of those remainders must be divisible by 3, so one of the numbers cannot be prime. This is a contradiction, so our assumption about the difference between the numbers must be wrong.

The proof for the other cases follows the same structure, and you can write a general proof that is true for all. This proof about primes in a sequence gives us a relationship linking primes theoretically. The difference between 97 primes linked together in an arithmetic sequence would have to be divisible by the product of all primes up to 97. This number would have more than 30 digits. At present mathematicians are unable to find an arithmetic sequence of 97 primes. This does not mean that one does not exist, as Lagrange's general proof covers all such large number cases. It just means that the search goes on.

Experiment time

Find arithmetic sequences involving primes

With lists of primes from Chapter M you can perform calculations using the theory above to find arithmetic sequences involving primes. Students enjoy searching for patterns in these seemingly random numbers.

Square numbers

Another one of Lagrange's great discoveries in number theory has to do with square numbers. In 1770 he proved that every positive integer is the sum of, at most, four square numbers. This means that I can write any number as a sum of squares:

$$13 = 3^2 + 2^2$$
$$14 = 3^2 + 2^2 + 1^2$$
$$15 = 3^2 + 2^2 + 1^2 + 1^2$$
$$16 = 4^2$$

This verifies that his idea works for these four numbers. Lagrange proved that whichever integer you choose, no matter how big, it will be the sum of, at most, four square numbers. The proof is quite long, so I will just indicate the path Lagrange took. Propositions demonstrated or assumed in proofs are called lemmas.

Lemma 1

Suppose that an odd prime, p, is a divisor of the sum of the squares of four integers, at least one of which is not divisible by p. Then p is the sum of four square numbers.

This takes three A4 pages to prove and uses, among other things, an interesting result found by Euler:

$$\left(x_0^2 + x_1^2 + x_2^2 + x_3^2\right)\left(y_0^2 + y_1^2 + y_2^2 + y_3^2\right) = z_0^2 + z_1^2 + z_2^2 + z_3^2$$

That is, if a number can be written as the sum of four square numbers, it can also be written as the product of two numbers, each of which can be written as the sum of four square numbers. This implies a recursive relationship. This means that as long as you can write some foundation numbers as the sums of square numbers, when these are multiplied together they will produce all the larger numbers as sums of four square numbers. What are these foundation numbers? Well, of course, they must be primes.

The second stage of the proof is to prove that it is true for all primes.

Lemma 2

Every prime number is the sum of four square numbers.

Again, the proof of this is long, but in the end it gives us the required result.

As with the arithmetic sequences, students will enjoy finding these square numbers. A good challenge for the students is to write down all the numbers up to 100 as the sum of no more than four square numbers.

Polygonal numbers

There are lots of special types of numbers, such as square numbers, and I will spend the rest of the chapter looking at these. First, I would like to tell you about how these special numbers came to be involved in my lessons. It started on the Isle of Wight. If you have ever been there you will know that some of the beaches have little shells scattered all over them. One summer I was taking a much needed rest from digging sandcastles and constructing moats when I heard a voice say, 'I'm bored, Dad'. Children's concentration span, even with plenty of sand to amuse them, tends to be limited. I had an idea to use all the wonderful resources around me. I suggested we made some triangular numbers using the shells as counters. In the classroom I've used plastic counters or just dots on squared paper. Here are the first few triangular numbers:

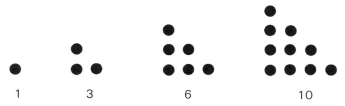

The nth triangular number is given by $t_n = \frac{1}{2}n(n+1)$.

Triangular numbers and other special numbers, called polygonal numbers, were first worked out and discussed by the ancient Greeks, particularly the Pythagoreans (see Chapter W).

You can prove that the sum of two consecutive triangular numbers is always a square number. A square number can be represented like this:

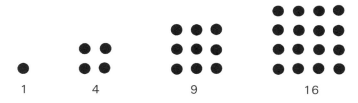

The nth square number is $s_n = n^2$.

Pentagonal numbers are:

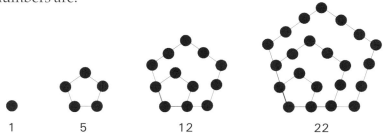

The nth pentagonal number is $p_n^5 = \frac{1}{2}n(3n-1)$. The superscript, 5, indicates that we are dealing with a five-sided shape. There is an interesting link between triangular, square and pentagonal numbers: $s_n + t_{n-1} = p_n^5$. For example, the third square number added to the second triangular number gives the 12 dots in the third pentagonal number. This formula is true for all n, and can be proved using algebra.

It can also be shown that every pentagonal number is one-third of a triangular number.

Hexagonal numbers also have a general formula, $p_n^6 = 2n^2 - n$, as do heptagaonal numbers, octagonal numbers, and so on. The general formula for any such number is:

$$p_n^m = \tfrac{1}{2}(m-2)n^2 - \tfrac{1}{2}(m-4)n$$

This, in turn, can be written in terms of triangular numbers as

$$p_n^m = t_n + (m-3)t_{n-1}$$

We worked for hours on the beach discovering many different connections between various groups of numbers, even reaching a point where we thought we had invented a new type of number. This is always a wonderful moment. I have used this idea of first-time discovery in many classroom situations to stimulate the students' interest and general mathematical development. This was illustrated in the Introduction, with Peter's method. I do not worry if the method is already known or if it is trivial. For the student who discovers it, it is a golden moment. Returning home from the beach I looked up star numbers, but unfortunately found that we were not the first to find the formula $*_n = s_n + 4t_{n-1}$.

Gauss and triangular numbers

Carl Friedrich Gauss was another great number theorist who produced many proofs. One of my favourites has to do with triangular numbers. On 10 July 1796, when he was 19 years old, he wrote in his diary, 'I have just proved this wonderful result that any natural number is the sum of three or fewer triangular numbers'. This result comes from the fact that any natural number of the form $8k + 3$ is the sum of the squares of three integers, which of course means that they must all be odd. So we can state

$$8k + 3 = (2a + 1)^2 + (2b + 1)^2 + (2c + 1)^2$$

Carl Friedrich Gauss
(1777–1855)

where a, b and c are non-negative integers. After some manipulation, the following result can be obtained:

$$k = \tfrac{1}{2}a(a+1) + \tfrac{1}{2}b(b+1) + \tfrac{1}{2}c(c+1)$$
$$= t_a + t_b + t_c$$

This proves the result, since k represents all natural numbers.

A good challenge is to write all the integers from 1 to 100 as sums of triangular numbers.

Indices, odds and ends

Here are a few odd results to do with indices, which I have always found interesting:

$$70^2 = 1^2 + 2^2 + 3^2 + \ldots + 24^2$$
$$3435 = 3^3 + 4^4 + 3^3 + 5^4$$
$$1634 = 1^4 + 6^4 + 3^4 + 4^4$$
$$1233 = 12^2 + 33^2$$

J. Kulik, born in 1773, spent 20 years of his life compiling a table of factors, up to 100 000 000. This just shows you that there are very many numbers out there and we know so little about them. My advice to you is to keep working, for you are bound to find out something new about numbers one day.

Further reference

Conway, J. and Guy, R. K. (1996) *The Book of Numbers*. New York: Copernicus.

Dickson, L. E. (1966) *History of the Theory of Numbers*. New York: Chelsea Publishing Company (originally published Washington: Carnegie Institution of Washington, 1919–1923).

Guy, R. K. (1994) *Unsolved Problems in Number Theory*. New York: Springer Verlag.

Roberts, J. (1996) *Lure of the Integers*. Cambridge: Cambridge University Press.

Sierpinski, W. (1988) *Elementary Theory of Numbers*, A. Schinzel (ed.). Amsterdam and New York: North-Holland.

J Jordan, Barnsley, Matrices and Ferns

Matrices have been around since 400BC and were first used by the Babylonians to help in the solution of problems involving simultaneous equations. This Babylonian work using matrices has been found recently, preserved on clay tablets. Yet the Babylonians merely used matrices as a device to store data, and not as a means of solving problems as we do today. It was not until the seventeenth century, some two thousand years later, that mathematicians were using matrices as tools to produce solutions to equations. Jordan takes his place in the history of matrices around 1869, with his work on the geometry of crystal structure. Along with his discoveries in this area, he proved that there are only four basic types of matrices from which all other matrices can be derived. These are called the Jordan forms of a matrix, and the four types have geometrical effects if applied to points in space.

Marie Ennemond Camille Jordan (1838–1922)

The four matrices relate to enlargement, shear, reflection and rotation, and are illustrated below.

Enlargement	Shear	Reflection	Rotation
$\begin{pmatrix} a & 0 \\ 0 & a \end{pmatrix}$	$\begin{pmatrix} a & 1 \\ 0 & b \end{pmatrix}$	$\begin{pmatrix} 0 & a \\ b & 0 \end{pmatrix}$	$\begin{pmatrix} a & -b \\ b & a \end{pmatrix}$

When you are watching a television programme such as *Top of the Pops*, and the pictures curl up into a cylinder or a sphere before tumbling out of view, you are watching matrices at work. To do this a computer remembers each coloured dot on the screen as a number. These numbers are then multiplied by the relevant matrix to produce the desired effect on the screen. This takes time, because the matrix multiplication becomes complex due to the number of calculations involved.

Experiment time

A fun way to get your students to practise matrix work is by using geometry. We cannot hope to do the number of calculations needed for changing a television screen, such as in the *Top of the Pops* example above. Yet with some graph paper and the help of a small

44

computer program, students can experiment with geometrical shapes and patterns in nature.

Thoughout this chapter I will be concentrating on rotation matrices, so let us look at a general rotation matrix:

$$R = \begin{pmatrix} \cos A & -\sin A \\ \sin A & \cos A \end{pmatrix}$$

With $A = 90°$, for example, we will produce the following rotation anti-clockwise on a triangle with vertices A, B and C at coordinates $(1, 2)$, $(2, 1)$ and $(1, 1)$.

$$\begin{array}{ccc} A & B & C \\ \end{array} \quad \begin{array}{ccc} A' & B' & C' \\ \end{array}$$

$$\begin{pmatrix} 0 & -1 \\ 1 & 0 \end{pmatrix} \begin{pmatrix} 1 & 2 & 1 \\ 2 & 1 & 1 \end{pmatrix} = \begin{pmatrix} -2 & -1 & -1 \\ 1 & 2 & 1 \end{pmatrix}$$

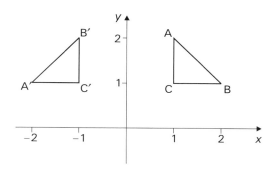

Applying the matrix R twice (in other words RR or R^2) gives:

$$\begin{array}{ccc} A' & B' & C' \\ \end{array} \quad \begin{array}{ccc} A'' & B'' & C'' \\ \end{array}$$

$$\begin{pmatrix} 0 & -1 \\ 1 & 0 \end{pmatrix} \begin{pmatrix} -2 & -1 & -1 \\ 1 & 2 & 1 \end{pmatrix} = \begin{pmatrix} -1 & -2 & -1 \\ -2 & -1 & -1 \end{pmatrix}$$

A good continuation to this is to ask the students what would happen to the shape if different types of rotations are used, for example rotations of 20° and 70°. In cases such as this the students will notice that they do not always get the expected result, because they will have rounded off the decimal values of the sine and cosine. This is very noticeable in cases when you use six 15° rotations, which should give a 90° rotation.

If the students have access to graphics calculators they will find the matrix functions useful in helping to improve their accuracy and speed calculations.

Up to this point we have only looked at rotations around the origin. If you want to rotate around a different centre point (x_0, y_0) you simply use the rotation matrix as above but with the centre coordinates subtracted from each coordinate. Then add the coordinates of the new centre to the result. The general formula looks like this:

$$\text{New value} = \begin{pmatrix} \cos A & -\sin A \\ \sin A & \cos A \end{pmatrix} \begin{pmatrix} x - x_0 \\ y - y_0 \end{pmatrix} + \begin{pmatrix} x_0 \\ y_0 \end{pmatrix}$$

For example, using the above equation with our example triangle and a centre of rotation at $(1, 1)$ we have $x_0 = 1$ and $y_0 = 1$. So we have:

$$\begin{pmatrix} 0 & -1 \\ 1 & 0 \end{pmatrix} \begin{pmatrix} 1-1 & 2-1 & 1-1 \\ 2-1 & 1-1 & 1-1 \end{pmatrix} = \begin{pmatrix} 0 & -1 \\ 1 & 0 \end{pmatrix} \begin{pmatrix} 0 & 1 & 0 \\ 1 & 0 & 0 \end{pmatrix}$$

$$= \begin{pmatrix} -1 & 0 & 0 \\ 0 & 1 & 0 \end{pmatrix}$$

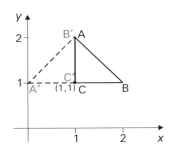

Adding the centre coordinates to each point gives $\begin{pmatrix} 0 & 1 & 1 \\ 1 & 2 & 1 \end{pmatrix}$.

So the new coordinates are $(0, 1)$, $(1, 2)$ and $(1, 1)$.

Students will need time to practise this type of rotation with a number of different types of shapes. I recommend using 90° rotations as above first, and then moving on to 180° and 270°. Other rotations using decimal matrices are possible with some students.

A good project for younger students is to get them to draw a simple rocket, aircraft or other such object, then perform a series of rotations with differing centres. These make excellent wall displays and this is a fun way for younger students to see geometry in action.

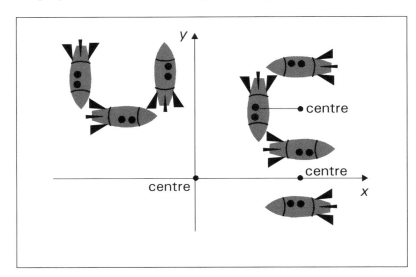

Extension ideas

Certain fractals (see Chapters D and F) can be generated from a series of random rotations. These types of fractals look like ferns and belong to a special category of fractal called iterated function systems. They were created by Michael Barnsley in 1985. Some developments in mathematics are difficult to understand, but with effort and hard work you can see how they were discovered. Others appear as if by magic from the magician's hat, and mere mortals can only look on in wonder at the work of a genius. Michael Barnsley's fern is one such development.

An example of Barnsley's fern fractal

Biologists have looked closely at Barnsley's ideas, as in nature the randomness used to generate these fern patterns would normally be a cause of death. When nature reproduces itself, it always appears to be ordered and structured with no random element. Yet Barnsley's method has points jumping around at random. Barnsley has claimed that the biologists were worrying for no reason at all, as his method only appears to be random, and under the surface there is a highly ordered mechanism at work. In his words:

the object itself does not depend on the randomness. With probability one, you always draw the same picture. It's giving deep information, probing fractal objects with a random algorithm. Just as, when we go into a new room, our eyes dance around it in some order which we might as well take to be random, and we get a good idea of the room. The room is just what it is. The object exists regardless of what I happen to do.

To produce this fern, Barnsley uses a rotation matrix, as we have used earlier in the chapter. The only difference is that after each rotation has produced a new set of points, these points are put back into the matrix and rotated again. The points are then plotted to produce a fern.

There is another slight complication to this method in that there is a random element to the process (see Chapter V). This is used to change some of the constants in the matrix to give more emphasis to the stem and main branches of the fern, as opposed to the finer edges.

Lets take a closer look at this process. Here is the basic matrix:

$$\text{new values} = \begin{pmatrix} a & b \\ d & e \end{pmatrix} \begin{pmatrix} x_{\text{old}} \\ y_{\text{old}} \end{pmatrix} + \begin{pmatrix} c \\ f \end{pmatrix}$$

You can see that the basic matrix is of the same form as the rotation matrix we used earlier. For Barnsley's fern we have the following sets of values for the constants:

	Set 1	Set 2	Set 3	Set 4
a	0.85	−0.15	0.2	0
b	0.04	0.28	−0.26	0
c	0	0	0	0
d	−0.04	0.26	0.23	0
e	0.85	0.24	0.22	0.16
f	1.6	0.44	1.6	0
Probability	0.85	0.07	0.07	0.01

Starting at the origin, point (0,0), we 'throw our dice', and look at the probability ranges given above. You need to use a random number generator to see which matrix set we use. One such random generator can be found on most calculators. For example, on a Casio scientific calculator it is the RAN# button, which gives a three-digit random number. Using $100 \times$ RAN# will give a two-digit integer part, which you can use to decide which set of constants to use in the matrix. If the two-digit integer is less than 86, use Set 1; if it falls between 86 and 92 (i.e. $100 \times (0.85 + 0.07)$), use Set 2, and so on.

It is a good idea for students to try generating the first few points on graph paper before using the computer. For example, if our random number generation means that we use Set 1, we use this matrix to rotate the origin point $(0, 0)$.

$$\begin{pmatrix} 0.85 & 0.04 \\ -0.04 & 0.85 \end{pmatrix}\begin{pmatrix} 0 \\ 0 \end{pmatrix} + \begin{pmatrix} 0 \\ 1.6 \end{pmatrix} = \begin{pmatrix} 0 \\ 1.6 \end{pmatrix}$$

We can plot the resulting point, $(0, 1.6)$, on graph paper, and then use the probability random number generator again. If we were to use Set 1 again on the new point $(0, 1.6)$, we would have:

$$\begin{pmatrix} 0.85 & 0.04 \\ -0.04 & 0.85 \end{pmatrix}\begin{pmatrix} 0 \\ 1.6 \end{pmatrix} + \begin{pmatrix} 0 \\ 1.6 \end{pmatrix} = \begin{pmatrix} 0.064 \\ 2.96 \end{pmatrix}$$

So we can plot the point $(0.064, 2.96)$ on the graph. Then suppose that the random number generation led us to use Set 3. We would get the following matrix:

$$\begin{pmatrix} 0.2 & -0.26 \\ 0.23 & 0.22 \end{pmatrix}\begin{pmatrix} 0.064 \\ 2.96 \end{pmatrix} + \begin{pmatrix} 0 \\ 1.6 \end{pmatrix} = \begin{pmatrix} -0.7568 \\ 2.265 \end{pmatrix}$$

So we now have the point $(-0.7568, 2.265)$ to plot on the graph. Notice how random these first few points are. You can continue this process but, as you can see, this method is not really intended to be done by hand. Investigating further into this process and finding the sorts of plants that Barnsley's method produces is best performed on the computer. Yet I think that some time spent at the start by the students plotting points helps to reinforce the process used by the computer. It also gives the students time to appreciate how amazing the method really is.

Computer support

- First run the program FERN to see one of these amazing pictures being created. Then students should alter the constants in the matrices in FERN to see the effect that this generates. These constants can be found on the following lines:

```
50   A(1)=0.85:A(2)=-0.15:A(3)=0.2:A(4)=0
60   B(1)=0.04:B(2)=0.28:B(3)=-0.26:B(4)=0
70   C(1)=0:C(2)=0:C(3)=0:C(4)=0
80   D(1)=-0.04:D(2)=0.26:D(3)=0.23:D(4)=0
90   E(1)=0.85:E(2)=0.24:E(3)=0.22:E(4)=0.16
100  F(1)=1.6:F(2)=0.44:F(3)=1.6:F(4)=0
```

For example, change the 0.85 in A(1) to 0.6 and then run the program again. Then change it back to 0.85 and change one of the other constants. Work systematically through them, making notes on the effects that the different letters have.

- Students can also change the probabilities required for each set. These are given on the following lines:

```
190  IF R<0.01 THEN K=4
200  IF R> 0.01 AND R<0.08 THEN K=3
210  IF R>0.08 AND R<0.15 THEN K=2
220  IF R>0.15 THEN K=1
```

What effects are seen when you reduce the Set 1 dominance of 0.85? What effect does each set of constants have on the whole fern? Reduce one probability to zero to find out.

- To create another plant structure try using the following numbers, or merely make up your own.

	Set 1	Set 2	Set 3	Set 4
a	0	0.2	–0.15	0.75
b	0	–0.26	0.28	0.04
c	0	0.23	0.26	–0.04
d	0.16	0.22	0.24	0.85
e	0	0	0	0
f	0	1.6	0.44	1.6
Probability	0.1	0.08	0.08	0.74

Further references

Barnsley, M. F. (1988) *Fractals Everywhere*. London: Academic Press.
Prusinkiewicz, P. *et al.* (1990) *The Algorithmic Beauty of Plants*. New York: Springer Verlag.
Stevens, P. (1974) *Patterns in Nature*. New York: Little, Brown.

See also:
www.astronomy.swin.edu.au/pbourke/fractals/fern/
http://Library.thinkquest.org/26242/full/types/ch4

K Kissing Circles

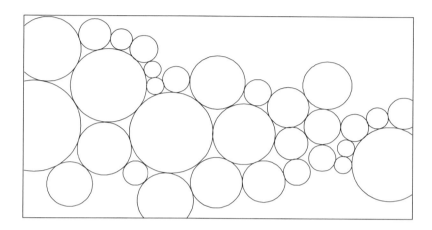

No one can doubt my words when I say that circles are special. Our clocks mark out the hours as the world turns full circle. Orbiting around us is the Moon, as we travel on a near circular path around the Sun, Sun and Moon looking to us like great circles moving slowly across the sky. When you marry you give circular bands of gold to signify your unending love. We talk of going full circle to make a journey complete. As you can imagine, the circle has always held an air of magic and mystery within human thought.

Experiment time

In 1936 the mathematician Frederick Soddy wrote a poem called 'The Kiss Precise' about four special circles. Here is one verse of it.

> Four circles to the kissing come.
> The smaller are the benter.
> The bend is just the inverse of
> The distance from the center.
> Though their intrigue left Euclid dumb
> There's now no need for rule of thumb.
> Since zero bend's a dead straight line
> And concave bends have minus sign,
> The sum of the squares of all four bends
> Is half the square of their sum.

(published in *Nature* **137**, 20 June, 1936)

The poem gives the general rule for drawing a fourth circle that touches three circles that are themselves touching. Using the last two lines of the extract we can write down the following formula, where B_1 is the 'bend' of circle 1, and so on:

$$B_1^2 + B_2^2 + B_3^2 + B_4^2 = \tfrac{1}{2}\left(B_1 + B_2 + B_3 + B_4\right)^2$$

Since the 'bend' is the inverse of the distance from the centre, it is given by the reciprocal of the radius.

$$B_1 = \frac{1}{r_1}$$

So you can write the above formula as:

$$\frac{1}{r_1^2} + \frac{1}{r_2^2} + \frac{1}{r_3^2} + \frac{1}{r_4^2} = \frac{1}{2}\left(\frac{1}{r_1} + \frac{1}{r_2} + \frac{1}{r_3} + \frac{1}{r_4}\right)^2$$

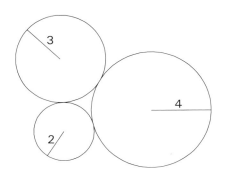

Drawing three circles with radiuses 2, 3 and 4 units, you can use the formula to find the radius of the final circle by solving the equation

$$\frac{1}{4} + \frac{1}{9} + \frac{1}{16} + \frac{1}{r^2} = \frac{1}{2}\left(\frac{1}{2} + \frac{1}{3} + \frac{1}{4} + \frac{1}{r}\right)^2$$

After some algebra this gives a quadratic equation with solutions $r = 0.418$ and $r = -7.056$. Notice that the poem gives us a clue that we should expect to obtain two solutions: 'concave bends have minus sign'. The positive answer is a small circle surrounded by the other three, and the negative answer means a larger circle surrounding the first three.

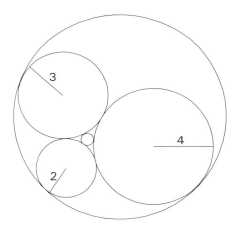

Students enjoy trying to find the fourth circle having drawn the first three using a pencil and compass. They can check their answers using the algebraic formula and obtain the exact solution. An interesting question to put to the students is 'Can all four radiuses have integer values?'

It is not just in recent times that circle formulas have been discovered. Over two thousand years ago the Greeks produced many interesting results. Here is just a small selection of them.

Pappus

The centres of the circles are at heights y_n above the horizontal diameter of the largest circle. If the radius of circle n is r_n, then the height of its centre is $y_n = 2nr_n$. By making each successive circle with a smaller radius you can create an interesting pattern. This sort of circular work, as well as practising geometrical skills, also creates great wall displays for the classroom.

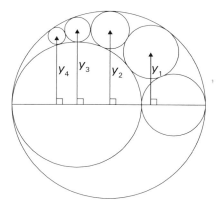

Archimedes

Buried away in the propositions of the *Book of Lemmas* by Archimedes are many intriguing theories concerning the *arbelos*, or shoemaker's knife, shown by the shaded area in the diagram.

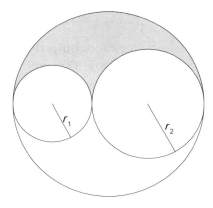

The shape has the following properties:

- The perimeter of the *arbelos* is the same as the circumference of the large circle enclosing the whole shape.
- The area of the *arbelos* is $\pi r_1 r_2$.
- The area of the *arbelos* is equal to the area of this shaded circle in the diagram.

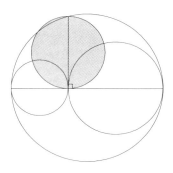

Euclid

Euclid's seven kissing circles can be constructed via the symmetries involved in the shape.

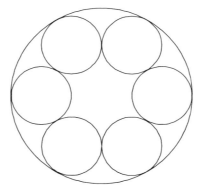

The method I have used with students is to divide the outer circle into six equal sectors.

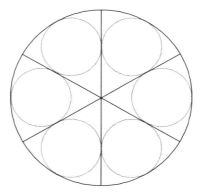

We know that the six circles lie in these sectors touching the outer circle. So to find out where they lie, divide one of these sectors in half and the circle's diameter must lie on this line. The circle must also touch the sector lines at just one point: a tangent. Look for the point where these perpendiculars cross to find the centre of each circle. Once the radius of one circle has been found all the others can be drawn.

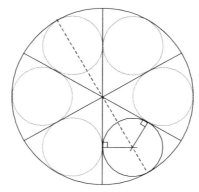

Having drawn the circles, it is interesting to calculate the radius of the largest circle that will fit in the central space in between the circles.

If you had eight, nine or more kissing circles, what pattern is formed by the radius of the largest circle to fit in each central space?

With some students I have found it better to start with five and six kissing circles, since the constructions are easier with the larger angles of 90° and 72°, respectively.

Further references

Heath, T. L. (1963) *A Manual of Greek Mathematics*. New York: Dover (originally published Oxford: Clarendon Press, 1931).

Ogilvy, C. S. (1969) *Excursions in Geometry*. New York: Oxford University Press.

Shively, L. S. (1939) *An Introduction to Modern Geometry*. New York: J. Wiley & Sons.

See also:
www.earthmeasure.com/
www.ics.unciedu/~eppstein/junkyard/sphere
www.libraryspot.com

L Life and John Conway

In 1970 John Conway invented the game Life. It is a game that he initially invented to be played on a draughts board, or some other such grid. The squares on the board are called cells. If there is a counter in a cell the cell is said to be alive; if there is no counter the cell is said to be dead. The rules of the game are:

1. A cell will remain alive if it has either two or three neighbours. Otherwise it will die.
2. Birth occurs when a cell has exactly three live neigbours.

British mathematician John Conway (1937–), inventer of the game Life

The game was popularised by Martin Gardiner in his then monthly column in *Scientific American* magazine.

In 1970 John Conway offered a $50 prize for anyone who came up with a Life pattern that grows without bounds. Computer programmers all over the world went to town trying to find new forms of Life. By now the idea of using a draughts board was lost, since the power of the computer allowed the game to be played very quickly. With the computer, Lifers could test out new Life forms and see their whole history in a very short period of time. It took Bill Gosper one month only to create the reproducing shape and collect the money. Pictured here is the Gosper Glider Gun, which is famous in Life circles. As this shape grows it shoots out small groups of cells, which Life addicts call gliders.

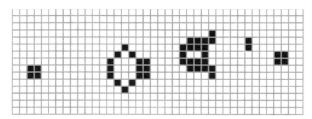

Gosper Glider Gun

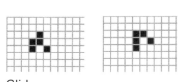

Gliders

Use the computer program GOSPER and you will see the gliders shooting out across the screen.

Martin Gardiner said 'My 1970 column on Conway's Life met with such an enthusiastic response among the computer world that their mania for exploring Life-forms was estimated to have cost the nation millions of dollars in illicit computer time'.

Some people became so fascinated that they began to wonder if they were watching something more than a game. Professor Ed Fredkin of the Massachusettes Institute of Technology said 'There was in fact the same sort, if more complex rules, behind the way insect and animals live. Maybe we ourselves are merely playing out the super game of Life played by some higher level being somewhere out there!'

John Conway continues to work on the idea of building a supercomputer that has a game of Life running inside it. The game of Life would control its processing and allow it to act in a more humanistic way, rather than the on/off computers that we use today. There is still an open question as to whether you can build a machine like this, since no one has proved it to be either possible or impossible.

Experiment time

In order to help students start their experiments, lets us bring back John Conway's initial idea of playing Life on a draughts board. This practical introduction allows the students to digest the rules of the game.

Certain initial configurations produce different sets of patterns. These can be grouped into four main categories: still, oscillator, glider and unbounded. These are interpreted as follows:

- **Still** – these cells do not change. In other words cells always have exactly two neighbours.
- **Oscillator** – these cells repeat a certain pattern over a given period.
- **Glider** – these cells flow through space maintaining the same shape.
- **Unbounded** – these cells grow larger for ever.

There are groups of cells that have a mixture of some or all of the above attributes. In the further references at the end of the chapter you will find websites that contain lists of all of the possible configurations that people have found over the past 30 years.

Let's start by looking at some simple examples that we can test using a few counters on a draughts board. Two counters, side by side, are lonely, since each has only one neighbour, so on the second turn they are both dead.

When we have three counters in a straight line, the two at each end only have one neighbour and so die on the second turn. The spaces above and below the middle cell each have three neigbours, so on the second turn we have two births. Then the process repeats itself producing the most simple oscillating Life form with a period of two.

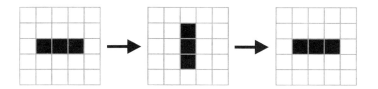

Here is another example of a simple oscillator with a period of two.

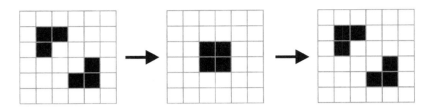

Here is a more complex oscillator with a period of two, and six cells in each phase of its life.

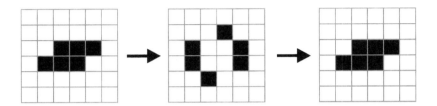

Still Life forms are patterns that do not change from one generation to the next. The general idea is that each counter only has two neighbours, and can therefore stay alive but not give birth to any more cells. A good challenge for students is to find the number of still Life forms that are possible using four, five, six, seven or more counters. Here are the first few:

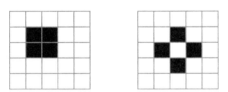

Two still Life forms with four cells   The unique five-cell still Life form

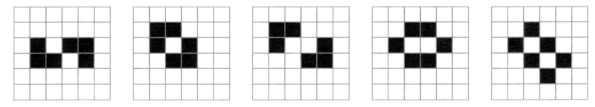

There are five still Life forms with six cells

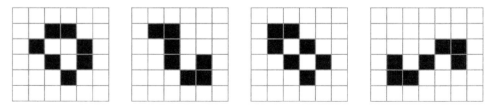

There are four still Life forms with seven cells

Beyond this you can find nine still Life forms with eight cells, ten with nine cells, and 25 with ten cells. If you are looking for more, the further references at the end of the chapter give you routes to follow.

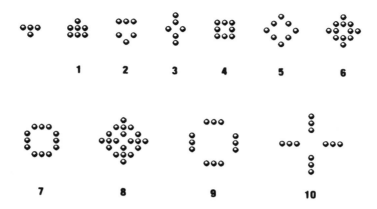

Starting with the four-cell shape above you reach a period two oscillator after ten moves. This Life shape is called the T tetromino and is very well ordered, unlike the deceptively simple-looking starting cell configuration given below, which has only one more cell than the T tetromino.

If you start to play Life with this one, you will find that it will grow and grow for ever, eventually creating a monster mess of a Life form. A good task for the students is to calculate the number of stages that can be fitted on a draughts board before it gets too big. To follow on they can run this on the computer to see what happens next.

Computer support

Using the computer program LIFE students can experiment with larger and more complex Life forms that exist and grow over many moves.

- Line

```
30    WINDOW (0,0)-(40,40)
```

gives the size of the axis used. At present it is set so the *x*- and *y*-axes have a range of 0 to +40. If you increase this range, then you must also increase the following lines:

```
40 DIM A%(45,45)
50 DIM B%(45,45)
70 N=40
```

- Line

  ```
  80 TT=14
  ```

  gives the number of moves in the game. At present it is set at 14.
- The following lines create the initial setup of cells on the screen

  ```
  150  A%(21,22)=1:PSET(21,22),4
  160  A%(22,22)=1:PSET(22,22),4
  170  A%(23,22)=1:PSET(22,22),4
  180  A%(22,21)=1:PSET(22,21),4
  ```

  These are set to give the T tetromino. If you want to run a different set of cells you need to change these lines. For example, to create the T tetromino monster with the extra cell, merely add the line

  ```
  151  A%(21,23)=1:PSET(21,23),4
  ```

If you don't want to keep looking at one particular Life form then the computer program LIFE2 allows you to enter the new cells you want each time it is used. Using axes in the range 0 to 40, get the students to draw out the pattern of cells on graph paper. With this program I have found it is best not to use more than ten cells. Once the cells have been entered, the program will allow you to choose the number of moves you want to make. Using Life like this is a good way to practise coordinates.

With both of these programs, as with GOSPER, if they run too fast and you cannot see what is happening then you will need to change line

```
350  FOR E= 1 TO 10000:NEXT E
```

Increase the 10000 to 100000, for example, and this will then slow the program down. The reason for this problem is that computers are just too quick!

Another alternative to my programs is to use one of the freeware downloads given in the further references at the end of the chapter. I recommend that you try LIFE32, as it is a highly developed package.

Here are a few of my favourites to help you start experimenting.

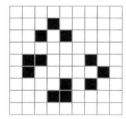

This one oscillates with period four, having 12, 18, 12 and 18 cells in each phase of its life.

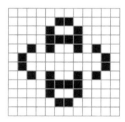

I also like this letter A shape, which has a period of six oscillations, with 28, 28, 32, 28, 28, 32 cells in each phase of its life.

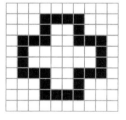

This period three oscillator was found to be the smallest of an infinitely large family of period three oscillators by Robert Wainwright.

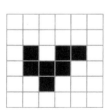

Run this one on the computer and after 148 generations it becomes a mixture of things, including three square blocks and two flowing gliders.

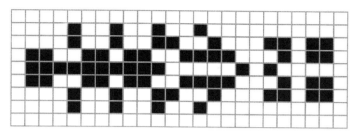

This monster is called a Two Glider Fuse. You need to see it in action: words cannot describe the event in all its glory.

Further references

Berlekamp, E. R. *et al.* (2001) *Winning Ways for your Mathematical Plays*, 2nd edn. Natick, MA: A.K. Peters.

Gardiner, M. (1983) *Wheels, Life, and Other Mathematical Amusements*. New York : W. H. Freeman.

Poundstone, W. (1985) *The Recursive Universe: Cosmic Complexity and the Limits of Scientific Knowledge*. Chicago, IL: Oxford University Press.

For a computer program to play Life see www.mindspring.com/~alanh/life/.

The best site to find hundreds of Life forms is www.treasure-troves.com/life

See also www.homes.uni-bielefeld.de/machim/goL

For freeware Life32 for Windows (see screen shot below), go to http://psoup.math.wisc.edu/Life32.html

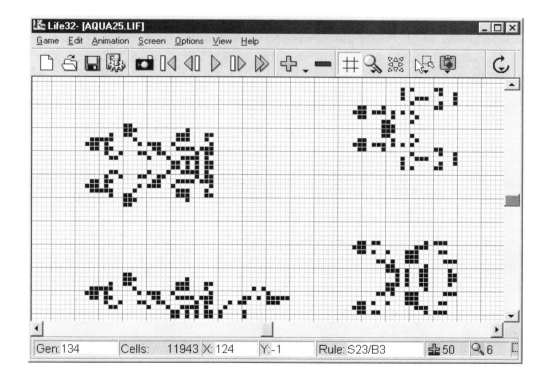

M Million Dollar Prizes and Prime Numbers

Professor G. H. Hardy (1877–1947) of Cambridge University, one of the greatest pure mathematicians of the twentieth century, once attempted to fool the mathematics community by claiming to have solved one of the most difficult problems in prime number theory: the Riemann Conjecture. The story begins during a taxi journey Hardy took to catch an ocean liner to Denmark, accompanied by his research student, Ramanujan (see Chapter R), who talked continually about his new prime number theories. By the time they reached the port the conversation had reached the Riemann Conjecture.

The great pure mathematician G. H. Hardy (1877–1947)

The Clay Mathematics Institute are offering a million dollars to anyone who can solve the Riemann Conjecture. With this sort of prize money you can guess that it is no simple task.

A conjecture is something that we believe to be true, although no one has yet been able to prove it. In 1860 Riemann conjectured that the real part of the solution to the following equation was always $\frac{1}{2}$. If this could be proved it would unlock the secret pattern in prime numbers. The equation can be written as an infinite arithmetic series of integer fractions to an unknown power s

$$0 = 1 + \frac{1}{2^s} + \frac{1}{3^s} + \frac{1}{4^s} + \frac{1}{5^s} + \dots$$

or as an infinite geometric series in primes

$$0 = \left(1 - \frac{1}{2^s}\right)^{-1} \left(1 - \frac{1}{3^s}\right)^{-1} \left(1 - \frac{1}{5^s}\right)^{-1} \left(1 - \frac{1}{7^s}\right)^{-1} \dots$$

To date nearly 1500 million solutions of this equation have been found. All have real part $\frac{1}{2}$, but no one can prove that this is always so.

Professor Hardy had worked on this proof for many years and had no success. The ocean liner suffered delays due to bad weather at sea, and he was told that the shipping company was waiting for storms to pass before their departure. Hardy seized his chance and sent a postcard to a colleague at Cambridge University saying that he had proved the Riemann Conjecture. He reasoned that if the liner sank on the journey and he died then he would have the fame of solving the problem. If the journey was fine then he could say that he had found a slight error in his solution. He survived the journey.

To date no one has solved the problem. It is one of the seven Millennium prize problems posed by the Clay Mathematics Institute. If you solve any of them they will give you one million dollars. This prize will be nothing compared to the fame and fortune of the prize winner, who would be deemed one of the greatest mathematicians that has ever lived.

Experiment time

If we are to have any hope of proving the Riemann Conjecture we need to know a little more about prime numbers. First, let us find a logical way of listing primes.

Eratosthenes' sieve

Eratosthenes was a Greek mathematician who was working at the library in Alexandra around 200BC when he discovered a method of listing primes. This method is called Eratosthenes's Sieve. Eratosthenes was very keen on all types of learning. His nickname was Philologus, or one who loves learning. Among his other claims to fame is the fact that he was the first person accurately to calculate the size of the Earth.

A prime number is a number greater than one, whose only divisors are one and the number itself. Numbers that are not prime are called composite and can be expressed as products of primes. Examples of primes are: 2, 3, 5, 7, 11, 13, 17, 19, 23, 29, 31, 37, 41, 43, 47, 53, 59, 61, 67, 71, 73, 79, 83, 89, 97, . . .

The Greek mathematician Eratosthenes of Cyrene (276BC–194BC)

Let's take a close look at Eratosthenes' Sieve and see the primes fall out.

First note that if a number is a composite such that $n = ab$, then a and b cannot both exceed $\sqrt{n}$. Therefore any composite integer n is divisible by a prime p that does not exceed $\sqrt{n}$. It follows from this that to test for primes it is only necessary to divide a number by natural numbers less than or equal to its square root. To find the primes from 2 to 30, we need only use the fact that $\sqrt{30} < 7$, and work with the primes 2, 3 and 5.

So list all the numbers 2–30:

2   3   4   5   6   7   8   9   10   11   12   13   14   15

16   17   18   19   20   21   22   23   24   25   26   27   28   29   30

Remove all multiples of 2, except for 2 itself

2   3   ~~4~~   5   ~~6~~   7   ~~8~~   9   ~~10~~   11   ~~12~~   13   ~~14~~   15

~~16~~   17   ~~18~~   19   ~~20~~   21   ~~22~~   23   ~~24~~   25   ~~26~~   27   ~~28~~   29   ~~30~~

Then remove all the multiples of 3, except for 3 itself

2   3   ~~4~~   5   ~~6~~   7   ~~8~~   ~~9~~   ~~10~~   11   ~~12~~   13   ~~14~~   ~~15~~
~~16~~   17   ~~18~~   19   ~~20~~   ~~21~~   ~~22~~   23   ~~24~~   25   ~~26~~   ~~27~~   ~~28~~   29   ~~30~~

Then repeat this with multiples of 5.

2   3   ~~4~~   5   ~~6~~   7   ~~8~~   ~~9~~   ~~10~~   11   ~~12~~   13   ~~14~~   ~~15~~
~~16~~   17   ~~18~~   19   ~~20~~   ~~21~~   ~~22~~   23   ~~24~~   ~~25~~   ~~26~~   ~~27~~   ~~28~~   29   ~~30~~

The remaining numbers are

2   3   5   7   11   13

   17   19   23   29

These are all the prime numbers from 2 to 30.

To check that students understand this idea, it is a good idea to get them to work out the prime numbers between 2 and 100.

Once they have done this divide the class into pairs, giving each pair a different group of one hundred numbers to work on – 100 to 200, 200 to 300, 300 to 400, etc. Working in pairs the students can check each other's work. Collect the data on the board and get the class to check for any composites that come out by accident. You can also use the program PRIMES, which lists prime numbers.

See if the class can spot any patterns in the long list of primes. You will be surprised at the good answers the students give.

How many primes are there?

In Book IX of *The Elements*, written in about 300BC, Euclid proved that there are infinitely many prime numbers. There may be infinitely many primes, but as yet no one has found a predictable pattern to link them all. Maybe now you are starting to see why people would want to list them, since without the list how can we look for patterns?

Let's look at Euclid's proof, which is a proof by contradiction. We first assume that what we want to prove is not true, then go on to show that this is not possible, hence finding out that our first assumption must have been wrong.

Euclid's proof

> Suppose that there are only a finite number of primes, the largest of which is p. We can construct the number $q = (2 \times 3 \times 5 \times \ldots \times p) + 1$, which consists of 1 added to all the primes up to p multiplied together.
>
> Clearly q is not divisible by any of 2, 3, 5, . . ., p, since these would all give a remainder of 1. So q is therefore either a prime or is divisible by a prime greater than p. In either case there is a prime greater than p, which is a contradiction.
>
> So there cannot be a finite number of primes. The number of primes must be infinite.

Primes are strange and wonderful things. Here are a few results and facts about primes for your students to test using all the primes they have collected.

- There are no primes between 370 261 and 370 373 or between 20 831 323 and 20 831 533. Get the students to look for the largest gap in the primes they have.
- Primes 13 331, 15 551, 16 661, 19 991 and 72 227 are examples of primes of the form *abbba*. Can the students find any patterns like this, or primes of the form *abbbbba*, such as 1 333 331, 1 777 771, 3 222 223 and 3 444 443? You can also get the students to test these to make sure they are prime.
- Twin primes are 3 and 5, 5 and 7, 11 and 13, 17 and 19, . . ., 1 000 000 000 061 and 1 000 000 000 063. How many twin primes do the students have in their list? How often do they occur? Do twin primes get rarer as the numbers get larger?
- For $n > 5$ there are at least two prime numbers between n and $2n$. Test to see if this is true for $n = 6, 7, 8, 9$ and so on.
- In 1919, Viggo Brun proved that the sum of the infinite series of twin primes given by

$$\sum \frac{1}{p} = \left(\frac{1}{3} + \frac{1}{5}\right) + \left(\frac{1}{5} + \frac{1}{7}\right) + \left(\frac{1}{11} + \frac{1}{13}\right) + \ldots$$

converges to 1.902 160 577 8 . . . .. This is called Brun's constant. Try this with the first few twin primes. Is the sum tending to this number?

Patterns in the frequency of primes

As the table shows, there seems to be some connection between the number of primes in the range of numbers 1 to n, and $n/\ln n$.

n	Range	Number of primes in range	$n/\ln n$
10	1–10	4	4.3
100	1–100	25	21.7
1000	1–1000	168	144.8
10 000	1–10000	1229	1086
10^5	1–10^5	9592	8686
10^6	1–10^6	78 498	72 382
10^7	1–10^7	664 579	620 420
10^8	1–10^8	5 761 455	5 428 681
10^9	1–10^9	50 847 534	48 254 942
10^{10}	1–10^{10}	455 052 511	434 294 482

This connection is called the prime number theorem and was proved to be true for large values of n in 1896 by Hadamard and Poussin. The proof entails the use of complex number theory applied to Riemann's zeta function. It was a glorious achievement for pure mathematicians, since many great figures in mathematical history, such as Gauss, Legendre, Chebyshev, and Riemann himself, had tried and failed to find patterns in prime numbers.

Extension ideas

- No one has found a formula to generate all primes, but there are some simple formulas to generate some primes. Test the following to see which primes they produce. Can you find any other equations that give primes?

  (a) $x^2 - x + 41$ gives primes for $x = 0, 1, 2, \ldots, 40$
  (b) $x^2 - 79x + 1601$ gives primes for $x = 0, 1, 2, \ldots, 79$
  (c) $x^2 + x + 17$ gives primes for $x = 1, 2, \ldots, 15$
  (d) $6x^2 + 6x + 31$ gives primes for $x = 0, 1, 2, \ldots, 28$

- In 1742, Christian Goldbach wrote to Euler (Chapter E) asking him if every positive even integer greater than 2 could be written as the sum of two primes. For example:

2+2 = 4	5+7 = 12
3+3 = 6	7+7 = 14
3+5 = 8	5+11 = 16
5+5 = 10	and so on

  This simple idea has turned out to be very difficult to prove. The publishers Faber and Faber have offered one million dollars to anyone who can prove this result. It is called the Goldbach Conjecture.

  The program GOLDBACH finds pairs of primes that sum to an even number and will help you to investigate this conjecture further.

Further references

Ribenboim, P. (1991) *The Little Book of Big Primes*. New York: Springer Verlag.
Ribenboim, P. (1995) *The New Book of Prime Number Records*, 3rd edn. New York: Springer Verlag.
Sierpinski, W. (1988) *Elementary Theory of Numbers*. New York: Elsevier Science.
Yuan, Wang (ed.) (1984) *Goldbach Conjecture*. River Edge, NJ, London and Singapore: World Scientific.

See also:
www.claymath.org
www-history.mcs.st-and.ac.uk/HistTopics/Prime-numbers.html
www.math.utah.edu/~alfeld/Eratosthenes

N Newton and Gravity

Born on Christmas Day, 1642, Sir Isaac Newton had one of the greatest ever mathematical minds. One of the most famous stories about him is one you may have heard, involving an apple. He was sitting having afternoon tea under his favourite apple tree in Woolsthorpe, when out of the blue an apple fell on his head. Apart from giving him a sore head, it also made him consider this question:

Could it be the same force responsible for both the apple falling and the Moon falling towards the Earth in its orbit?

He set to work that afternoon and mathematically confirmed that it was the same force acting in both of these situations: the force due to gravity. He then asked the question:

If it were true for these bodies, could it not be true for all things, such as planets and asteroids; in fact, universally true?

The famous English mathematician, Sir Isaac Newton (1642–1727)

When he had found out that it was universally true he wrote down all his ideas, checking carefully to make sure that he had not made any errors. Then he did a very strange thing. He put all this work away and did not tell anyone about his discoveries. Various explanations have been put forward to explain Newton's reasons for not telling the world, but in reality no one really knows why he did this. Some say he was worried about the fame it would bring, as he greatly valued his privacy. In fact, he kept this wonderful discovery secret for 20 years, finally publishing the complete theory in *Principia Mathematica* in 1686. This book caused great controversy. The church felt that the order in the heavens was created by God and man should leave such matters alone. The general scientific community found it difficult to believe that gravitation could be affecting things at such distances with no connections between them. Questions such as 'Where are the ropes pulling these planets together?' were asked.

There was also talk from pseudoscientists that love's great power was related to Newton's laws and the reason we fall in love can be explained by these laws! Headlines in the tabloid newspapers of the time announced 'We are just bodies forced to be attracted to each other by Newton's gravitational interactions' and 'Love is a gravitational Law!'

Throughout his life it was clear that Newton was a man who loved to know the unknown. In his lifetime he was a giant, like Einstein is today. Even after all these years, we marvel at the wonder of his great insight into mathematics and the natural world.

Experiment time

We learn about the way things fall from our earliest days playing with toys and watching how they move. Plants also know about gravity, and send their roots down and shoots up, feeling out gravity's path. If you put a plant in a rotating basket its roots will grow towards the centre as the acceleration is greatest in that direction.

What is gravity? This is a good question, and one for which I have no answer. No one has the answer. Newton told us how it affects other bodies, but what machinery lies inside it is a question for the great minds of the future. It is an immensely important question to answer, as its solution would solve the mystery of mass. Mass is the stuff that we, and the universe, are made of, but what is it?

Acceleration due to gravity

Galileo Galilei (1564–1642) was the first to show that all bodies fall at the same speed, regardless of size or weight. This idea would have been known to Newton and may have helped him to calculate the value of gravity. Galileo's experiment involved dropping weights from the top of the leaning tower of Pisa. To perform this experiment he tied five weights to a long string, where the distances between the weights were in the ratio 1:3:5:7. When the string was dropped, and the weights fell and hit the ground, the intervals between the noises they made when they hit the ground were the same. This illustrated that all weights fall at constant acceleration. This rate is what we call gravity. You do not need to go all the way to Pisa to do this experiment, as you can repeat it by tying five coins to a piece of thread in the ratio given above.

The distances that the weights fell were in the ratio 1:4:9:16. This can be calculated using the formula $x = \frac{1}{2}gt^2$ since for time, t, equal to 1, 2, 3 and 4, you get distances $\frac{1}{2}g$, $2g$, $\frac{9}{2}g$ and $8g$, respectively. These are the distances, x, through which the weight falls every second, falling with the acceleration due to gravity given by the gravitational constant, g.

Using these ratios get your students to calculate the time for their weights to hit the ground from different heights. In this free-fall case, g is approximately 9.81 m s^{-2}. This is an acceleration, so gravity acts to speed up the motion of each weight as it falls. As the weight falls towards the ground it will fall faster and faster until something breaks its fall.

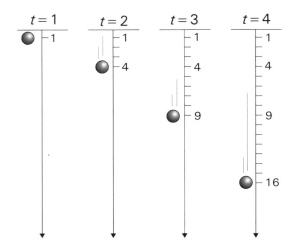

The numerical value of the acceleration due to gravity

You can check the numerical value of the acceleration due to gravity by rolling a ball down an inclined plane. You will need a stainless steel ball that is highly polished, so as to avoid frictional forces, and a 30 cm ruler that has a groove down the centre. Incline the ruler at a very small angle so as to allow the ball to roll slowly down the slope. Then time how long it takes for the ball to get to the end of the 30 cm ruler, and note the angle that the ruler makes with the horizontal.

Using the formula

$$g = \frac{84}{t^2 \sin A}$$

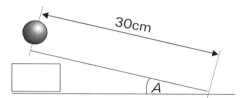

you can calculate the value of the gravitational constant.

Note also that for small angles the ball should travel through 2 cm, 6 cm, 13 cm and 23 cm at approximately 1, 2, 3 and 4 seconds, respectively.

Greater accuracy in the approximation

To obtain greater accuracy for this approximation to the numerical value of the acceleration due to gravity, you need to perform a more complex experiment. As you will have noticed, the greatest error in the above experiment is human error in the timing of the fall. To avoid this you need to use an automatic electric timer. You will need an electromagnet, a metal ball and an electronic clock. I have never had a problem obtaining this equipment from the physics department in the school, and, in fact, they usually want to be involved. The experiment becomes truly cross-curricular.

Set the apparatus up as shown in the circuit diagram.

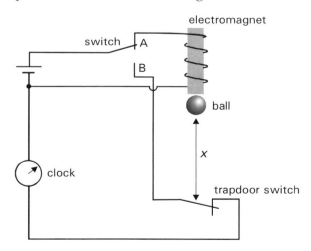

The circuit sends electricity into the electromagnet to hold the ball in place. When the switch is moved to B, the magnet is switched off and the ball falls. At the same moment as the ball is released, the electric circuit is completed to the clock, so it starts timing. When the ball hits the trapdoor switch this breaks the circuit to the clock, thus giving the time for the fall.

Students can use this apparatus to record the times for the distances shown in the table.

Distance, x, in metres	0.1	0.15	0.2	0.25	0.3
Time, t, in seconds					

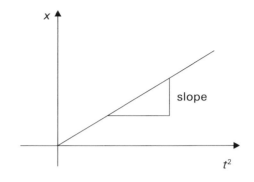

The values of distance and time are linked by the relationship $x = \frac{1}{2}gt^2$, so by plotting the graph x against t^2, students will obtain a straight line with a slope of $\frac{1}{2}g$. Multiplying the value of the slope by 2 will give a value for g very close to 9.81 m s^{-2}.

A water experiment

Another way to find the gravitational constant, g, is with water. As a stream of water flows from a tap, you will notice that the flow gets thinner, until it reaches a stage where it starts to break up. The thinning is due to the fact that as it falls it is accelerating, due to gravity. Since the volume of water flowing out of the tap is constant, the volume of water at any level must also be constant. As it speeds up, the cross-sectional area of the stream of water is reduced.

The students need to be in pairs to do this experiment, as one will be collecting data while the other is doing calculations. To start with, the students need to calculate the flow rate from the tap. This can be done by seeing how long it takes to fill a 250 cm^3, or quarter of a litre, flask. This should take a few seconds, and gives you the flow rate per second (F cm^3 s^{-1}).

Next, measure the diameter of the flow at the tap. From this you can calculate the speed of the water as it comes out of the tap.

$$\text{Area of flow from tap} = A_1 = \pi\left(\frac{d_1}{2}\right)^2 \text{cm}^2$$

$$\text{Speed from tap} = \frac{F}{A_1} = v_1 \text{ cm s}^{-1}$$

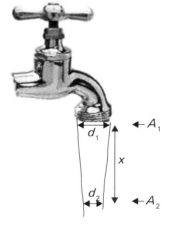

Then measure the diameter and height below the tap of another point in the flow, before the water starts to break up.

$$\text{Area of flow from tap} = A_2 = \pi\left(\frac{d_2}{2}\right)^2 \text{cm}^2$$

$$\text{Speed from tap} = \frac{F}{A_2} = v_2 \text{ cm s}^{-1}$$

Then you can calculate an approximate value for gravity from the equation

$$g = \frac{v_2^2 - v_1^2}{2x}$$

This process may seem long, but there are a lot of good approximation skills to be learnt by the students in performing this experiment. To clarify the method, I will give you an example of the results you might obtain.

A flow rate of $250\,\text{cm}^3$ in 5 seconds gives F = $\frac{250}{5}$ = $50\,\text{cm}^3\text{s}^{-1}$.

$$A_1 = \pi(0.7)^2 = 1.5\,\text{cm}^2$$

$$v_1 = \frac{50}{1.5} = 33\tfrac{1}{3}\,\text{cm}\,\text{s}^{-1} = \frac{1}{3}\,\text{m}\,\text{s}^{-1}$$

$$A_2 = \pi(0.35)^2 = 0.35\,\text{cm}^2$$

$$v_2 = \frac{50}{0.35} = 143\,\text{cm}\,\text{s}^{-1} = 1.43\,\text{m}\,\text{s}^{-1}$$

$$\therefore g = \frac{(1.43)^2 - (0.35)^2}{2 \times 0.10} = 9.612\,\text{m}\,\text{s}^{-2}$$

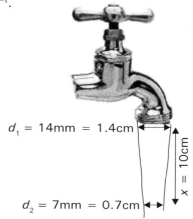

d_1 = 14mm = 1.4cm

d_2 = 7mm = 0.7cm

x = 10cm

Further references

Christianson, G. E. (1984) *In the Presence of the Creator: Isaac Newton and His Times*. New York: Free Press and London: Collier Macmillan.

Feynman, R. P. and Phillips, R. (1992) *The Character of Physical Law*. Harmondsworth: Penguin.

Newton, I. (1999) *The Principia: Mathematical Principles of Natural Philosophy by Isaac Newton*, I. Bernard Cohen and Anne Whitman (trans.). Berkeley, CA: University of California Press.

See also
www.user.globalnet.co.uk/~thf/newton

O Odd, Even and Fibonacci Numbers

Odd numbers: $1, 3, 5, 7, 9, 11, \ldots, 2n + 1$
Even numbers: $2, 4, 6, 8, 10, 12, \ldots, 2n$

Odd and even integers are the basic building blocks of our number system. We owe this to Leonardo of Pisa, better known as Fibonacci, who is first credited with introducing this system to Europe in 1202. This number system is the Hindu-Arabic way of counting and before Fibonacci publicised this in his *Book of the Abacus* (*Liber abaci*), Europeans were still counting in Roman numerals. Yet history remembers him not for this extremely useful contribution to European mathematics, but for a sequence of numbers that we now call the Fibonacci sequence:

The Italian mathematician Leonardo of Pisa (c. 1170–1250), who is better known as Fibonacci

$$1, 1, 2, 3, 5, 8, 13, 21, 34, 55, \ldots$$

The nineteenth-century French mathematician Édouard Lucas (see Chapter H) investigated the numbers in the Fibonacci sequence (Fibonacci numbers) in great detail. There are both odd and even numbers in the sequence. To find the next number in the sequence merely add the previous two. The mathematical formula for this sequence is $F_n = F_{n-1} + F_{n-2}$. For example,

$$F_3 = F_2 + F_1 = 1 + 1 = 2$$
and $$F_{11} = F_{10} + F_9 = 55 + 34 = 89$$

Fibonacci numbers have intrigued mathematicians for centuries, mainly owing to the fact that they occur in a multitude of interesting and strange places, one of the strangest being biology. If you count seeds and petals in flowers such as sunflowers, daisies, pineapples and pine cones, you will find that the resulting numbers are all Fibonacci numbers.

There is also a link with the special number called the golden ratio:

$$\tau = \tfrac{1}{2}\left(1 + \sqrt{5}\right) = 1.61803\ldots$$

The golden ratio is said to have pleasing properties to the eye. In art and architecture over the centuries many artists have used this ratio in their work. One of the definitions of the golden ratio comes from the rectangle. A rectangle is said to be golden if a smaller rectangle

72

of similar shape is left when a square that fits the shorter side is removed, as shown in the diagrams below:

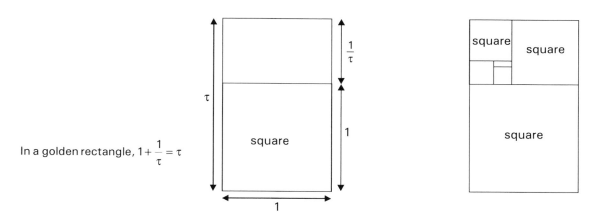

In a golden rectangle, $1 + \dfrac{1}{\tau} = \tau$

Another definition of the golden ratio can be obtained from these triangles:

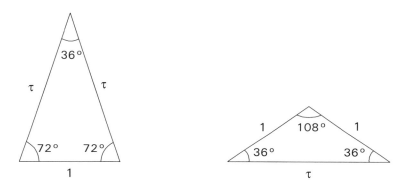

Experiment time

Let us experiment with Fibonacci numbers to illustrate some of the patterns that can be found.

Ratios

A good place to start is to look at the ratios of consecutive Fibonacci numbers. They are alternately greater or less than the golden ratio. For example:

$$\frac{1}{1} = 1 \qquad\qquad \frac{5}{3} = 1.666\ldots$$

$$\frac{2}{1} = 2 \qquad\qquad \frac{8}{5} = 1.6$$

$$\frac{3}{2} = 1.5 \qquad\qquad \frac{13}{8} = 1.625$$

Note that as we progress through the numbers the ratio gets closer to the golden ratio, and eventually will, in the limit, be $\tau = \frac{1}{2}\left(1 + \sqrt{5}\right) = 1.61803\ldots$.

Solving $F_n = F_{n-1} + F_{n-2}$

The equation $F_n = F_{n-1} + F_{n-2}$ can be solved by substituting $F_n = x^n$ to give $x^{n-2}(x^2 - x - 1) = 0$. By solving this quadratic equation $x^2 - x - 1 = 0$ you can find two roots, which are the key parts of the general formula for a Fibonacci number:

$$F_n = \frac{1}{\sqrt{5}}\left[\left(\frac{1+\sqrt{5}}{2}\right)^n - \left(\frac{1-\sqrt{5}}{2}\right)^n\right]$$

From this formula you can work out any number in the Fibonacci sequence exactly. For example, if you wanted to find the tenth number in the sequence, let $n = 10$ in the above formula. This is a good way to look at large Fibonacci numbers without having to work out the whole sequence. It is a good calculator exercise for students to use this formula to find a list of Fibonacci numbers. This list will be useful in the next exercise.

Fibonacci Nim

Fibonacci Nim is a game is played by two players. Each player takes turns writing down Fibonacci numbers to subtract from a predetermined total. The aim is to be the first to reach zero.

Any number can be expressed as the sum of Fibonacci numbers.

For example, $40 = 34 + 5 + 1$, or $31 = 21 + 8 + 2$, or $54 = 34 + 13 + 5 + 2$.

This is an interesting fact that students should check before beginning the game. Having confirmed this fact the students will be better equipped to play the game, since they will have familiarised themselves with Fibonacci numbers.

The first player is allowed to subtract any Fibonacci number that is less than the total. The Fibonacci number that the second player subtracts must be less than twice the first player's selection. From then on the players take it in turns to pick at least one Fibonacci number to subtract, but the sum of the numbers they choose must not be more than twice the preceding sum subtracted. The first player to reach zero wins.

For example, start with 50. Player A subtracts 8, leaving 42. Player B can subtract up to 2×8, so subtracts 13. This leaves 29. Player A can subtract a total up to $2 \times 13 = 26$, so takes 8 and 13, leaving 8. Player B then takes 8 and wins the game.

The strategy to use to win is as follows. If the total of the numbers remaining is not a Fibonacci number then it can be expressed as the sum of Fibonacci numbers. The player subtracts any number of small Fibonacci numbers from the total remaining, provided that their sum is less than half the next number in the sequence. Thus from $54 = 34 + 13 + 5 + 2$, the player would take only 2, not $2 + 5$ since $2 \times (2 + 5) > 13$, and the next player could take 13 and leave 34, which is a number in the sequence.

Once students are familiar with the Fibonacci sequence they find this game challenging. The start number can be any number other than a Fibonacci number, but beginners should keep to under 100.

Extension ideas

- Which of the Fibonacci numbers are even? Students will find that it is every third number in the sequence. Can they prove this for all Fibonacci numbers?
- The sum of any ten consecutive Fibonacci numbers is equal to 11 times the seventh. Students can verify that this is true and then prove it with algebra.
- The sum of Fibonacci numbers squared is equal to the last number in the sequence multiplied by the next. As a formula this statement can be written

$$F_1^2 + F_2^2 + F_3^2 + \ldots + F_n^2 = F_n F_{n+1}$$

Taking the first six Fibonacci numbers, for example,

$$1^2 + 1^2 + 2^2 + 3^2 + 5^2 + 8^2 = 8 \times 13$$

Is this always true?

- The following equations are true for all Fibonacci numbers:

$$F_{n+3}F_n - F_{n+2}F_{n+1} = (-1)^n$$

$$F_{n+1}^2 - F_n F_{n+2} = (-1)^{n+1}$$

With all of these relationships for Fibonacci numbers, students will be able to check to ensure that they work in particular cases. Some students will enjoy the challenge of trying to prove that they work in every case.

Further references

Huntley, J. E. (1970) *The Divine Proportion: A Study in Mathematical Beauty*. New York: Dover Publications.

Kepler, J. (1966) *The Six-Cornered Snowflake*, L. L. Whyte (trans.), C. Hardie (ed.). Oxford: Oxford University Press (originally published in 1611).

Vajda, S. (1989) *Fibonacci and Lucas Numbers, and the Golden Section: Theory and Applications*. Chichester: E. Horwood and New York: Halsted Press.

Vorobév, N. N. (1961) *Fibonacci Numbers*, H. Moss (trans.), I. N. Sneddon (ed.). Oxford and New York: Pergamon Press.

See also:
www.mcs.surrey.ac.uk/Personal/R.Knott/Fibonacci

For online versions of Fibonacci Nim see:
www.cit.gu.edu.au/teaching/CIT1104/examples/FNim/Applet/example1.html
www.stat.ucla.edu/~tom/Games/fibonim.html

P Pi or π

Pi = 3.	1415926535	8979323846	2643383279	5028841971	6939937510
	5820974944	5923078164	0628620899	8628034825	3421170679
	8214808651	3282306647	0938446095	5058223172	5359408128
	4811174502	8410270193	8521105559	6446229489	5493038196
	4428810975	6659334461	2847564823	3786783165	2712019091
	4564856692	3460348610	4543266482	1339360726	0249141273
	7245870066	0631558817	4881520920	9628292540	9171536436
	7892590360	0113305305	4882046652	1384146951	9415116094
	3305727036	5759591953	0921861173	8193261179	3105118548
	0744623799	6274956735	1885752724	8912279381	8301194912
	9833673362	4406566430	8602139494	6395224737	1907021798
	6094370277	0539217176	2931767523	8467481846	7669405132
	0005681271	4526356082	7785771342	7577896091	7363717872
	1468440901	2249534301	4654958537	1050792279	6892589235
	4201995611	2129021960	8640344181	5981362977	4771309960
	5187072113	4999999837	2978049951	0597317328	1609631859
	5024459455	3469083026	4252230825	3344685035	2619311881
	7101000313	7838752886	5875332083	8142061717	7669147303
	5982534904	2875546873	1159502863	8823537875	9375195778
	1857780532	1712268066	1300192787	6611195909	2164201989

These are the first 1000 decimal digits of pi (π) arranged in groups of 50 digits.

How far is it round a circle? How far does a wheel travel in rolling one revolution? The answer in each case, of course, involves π. The circumference of a circle is equal to π times the diameter.

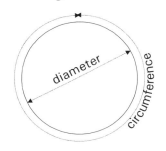

What is π? Since π turns up in so many areas of mathematics, some say that there is a deeper reason for this number's existence than merely to tell us the circumference of a circle. There is a story illustrating just this point as follows:

No matter how mathematics is approached, π forms an integral part. In his book Budget of Paradoxes, *Augustus De Morgan illustrates how little the usual definition of π suggests its origin. He was explaining to an actuary what the chances were at the end of a given time that a certain proportion of a group of people would be alive. He quoted the formula employed by actuaries which involves π. On hearing the geometric meaning of π, the actuary, who had been listening with interest, interrupted and exclaimed, 'My dear friend, that must be a delusion. What can a circle have to do with the number of people alive at the end of a given year?'*

In Chapter B we saw that π appears in the probability experiment, and there may be no area of mathematics that is not invaded by its presence. So what is π?

Experiment time

The earliest estimates for the value of π can be traced back to the Egyptians, who used a value of $4\left(\frac{8}{9}\right)^2 = 3.1605$. The Babylonians used a slightly better approximation of $\frac{25}{8} = 3.125$. It was Archimedes (see Chapter A) who, by calculating the perimeters of two regular 96-sided polygons, one inscribed and the other exscribed on a circle of unit diameter, was able to calculate the following range for π: $3\frac{10}{71} < \pi < 3\frac{1}{7}$.

Archimedes' method for approximating π

Archimedes' method for approximating π can be repeated in the classroom. Start by using two squares with a unit circle as shown here. The external square has a perimeter of 4 units. The internal square's perimeter is $\frac{4}{\sqrt{2}} = 2.82842\ldots$, giving the range for π as $2.82842 < \pi < 4$.

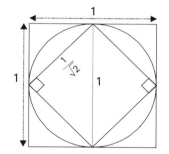

This first approximation for π can gradually be improved upon by increasing the size of the polygons. Once you get to hexagons and octagons the approximation of π is quite accurate.

Let's look at the method of constructing a hexagon around the circle. First divide the circle into six equal parts by drawing three lines through the centre of the circle. The intersections with the circle will create the internal hexagon, as shown in the diagram. Then find the midpoint of each side of the internal hexagon and draw out from the centre of the circle through the midpoints. The external hexagon will be a tangent to the circle at the point where the internal hexagon touches the circle.

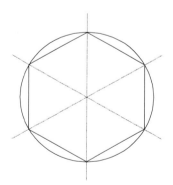
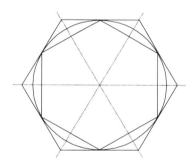

There are many other ways of estimating π. Before we look at these, you might wonder why we want to. Well, the reason is that π is the most famous and remarkable of all numbers, as it is transcendental and irrational. This means that no algebraic equation can found which has π as its solution, and no pattern can be found in its decimal digits. In 1800 Legendre proved that π was irrational. It took another eighty years for the mathematician Lindermann to prove that it was transcendental.

An algorithm to estimate π

Even after all these proofs there are still mathematicians who want to see if there could be a pattern. To find a pattern you would need to statistically analyse the digits in π, and to do this well you need a large number of digits. In July 1997, Professor Y. Kanada at the University of Tokyo calculated π to 5.15396×10^{10} decimal digits. This took 29 hours of computing time, on a fast computer! He used the algorithm below, which has the amazing property that the number of correct digits for π approximately doubles with each loop of the algorithm that you perform.

To calculate π using the algorithm start at the first step and go through to the end in order. Then go back to the start with your new values and repeat the process. The print line shows the approximation to π.

Initial values are $x = n = 1$, $y = \frac{1}{\sqrt{2}}$ and $z = \frac{1}{4}$.

10    $m = x$

$$x = \frac{x+y}{2}$$

$$y = \sqrt{ym}$$

$$z = z - n(x-m)^2$$

$$n = 2n$$

PRINT $\dfrac{(x+y)^2}{4z}$

GOTO 10

Try this algorithm using your calculator and you will see how quick it is. If you code this on to your computer you need to think about how to show more than 16 digits on the screen.

After 29 hours and 5.15396×10^{10} digits, Professor Kanada found that the digit 8 appeared slightly more frequently than the other digits. This indicates that a pattern might exist, and π might not be as special as we used to think. Mathematicians are still working on this possibility.

But why worry about calculating it when π correct to 39 decimal places is sufficient to compute the circumference of the visible universe to the accuracy of a hydrogen atom? Would you really ever need more precision than that?

Using Microsoft Excel to estimate π

Using MS Excel allows us to estimate π in a different way.

A circle of radius one unit has an area π, so the ratio of the area of the circle to the area of the squire is $\frac{\pi}{4}$. Using the random number generator in MS Excel we can create random dots inside the square. Some of these will be inside the circle and others not, but if they are placed truly at random (see Chapter V) then there is an equal probability that they will be anywhere inside the square. So the chance of being inside the circle is $\frac{\pi}{4}$. In other words to estimate π we need only count the dots – or let MS Excel count them for us! Once you find the ratio of dots that are inside the circle to those that are inside the square, multiplying this by 4 will give an estimate for π.

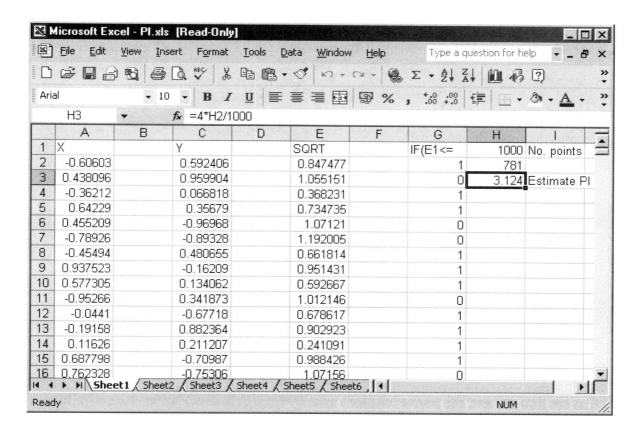

The screen shot shows the suggested worksheet layout with the following formulas:

Cell	Formula	Purpose
A2	=RAND( )*2 -1	Random number x, from –1 to +1
C2	=RAND( )*2 -1	Random number y, from –1 to +1
E2	=SQRT(A2^2+C2^2)	Distance from origin
G2	=IF(E2<=1,1,0)	If point is inside circle
G1003	=SUM(G2:G1001)	Count number of points in circle
G1005	=PI( )	Display actual value of π

With a Pentium processor the calculation is done extremely quickly. Why not try increasing the number of cells to improve the accuracy of the approximation? On the CD you will find the MS Excel file PI used above.

Extension ideas

- Gregory's series

$$\frac{\pi}{4} = 1 - \frac{1}{3} + \frac{1}{5} - \frac{1}{7} + \ldots + (-1)^n \frac{1}{2n+1}$$

  can be used to find an estimate for π. Multiply both sides by 4 and start the slow process of adding and subtracting terms. This is derived from the Taylor series (see Chapter T).

- Using the relations

$$\tan^{-1} x + \tan^{-1} y = \frac{\pi}{4} \quad \text{and} \quad \tan(A+B) = \frac{\tan A + \tan B}{1 - \tan A \tan B}$$

  you can obtain the equation

$$\frac{x+y}{1-xy} = 1.$$

  Euler (see Chapter E) used these equations to obtain the following relation for π:

$$\tan^{-1}\left(\tfrac{1}{2}\right) + \tan^{-1}\left(\tfrac{1}{3}\right) = \frac{\pi}{4} \quad \text{with } x = \tfrac{1}{2} \text{ and } y = \tfrac{1}{3}.$$

  Verify this by ensuring that these values of x and y satisfy the above equations. Can you find any other values of x and y that would also satisfy these equations?

- One of the most accurate relations for π is

$$4\tan^{-1}\left(\tfrac{1}{5}\right) - \tan^{-1}\left(\tfrac{1}{239}\right) = \frac{\pi}{4}$$

  To verify this you will need to use the equation for $\tan 4A$.

- A good calculator exercise for students is to find the degree of accuracy of the following formulas and estimates approximating π:

  (a) $\quad \frac{22}{7}$

  (b) $\quad \frac{377}{120}$

  (c) $\quad \frac{355}{113}$

  (d) $\quad \frac{103993}{33102}$

  (e) $\quad \pi = 2\sqrt{2}\left(1 + \tfrac{1}{3} - \tfrac{1}{5} - \tfrac{1}{7} + \tfrac{1}{9} + \tfrac{1}{11} - \tfrac{1}{13} - \tfrac{1}{15} + \ldots\right)$

  (f) $\quad \dfrac{\pi-3}{4} = \dfrac{1}{2\times3\times4} - \dfrac{1}{4\times5\times6} + \dfrac{1}{6\times7\times8} - \ldots$

  (g) $\quad \dfrac{\pi^2}{6} = 1 + \dfrac{1}{2^2} + \dfrac{1}{3^2} + \dfrac{1}{4^2} + \ldots$

(h) $\quad \dfrac{\pi^2}{6} = \dfrac{2^2}{2^2 - 1} \times \dfrac{3^2}{3^2 - 1} \times \dfrac{5^2}{5^2 - 1} \times \dfrac{7^2}{7^2 - 1} \times \ldots$

(i) $\quad \pi = 2\left(\frac{2}{1} \times \frac{2}{3} \times \frac{4}{3} \times \frac{4}{5} \times \frac{6}{5} \times \frac{6}{7} \times \ldots\right)$

(j) $\quad \pi = \left(9^2 + \frac{19^2}{22}\right)^{\frac{1}{4}}$

(k) $\quad \pi = \dfrac{63\left(17 + 15\sqrt{5}\right)}{25\left(7 + 15\sqrt{5}\right)}$

(l) $\quad \pi = \dfrac{99^2}{2206\sqrt{2}}$

(m) $\quad \pi = \displaystyle\sum_{n=0}^{\infty} \dfrac{1}{16^n}\left(\dfrac{4}{8n+1} - \dfrac{2}{8n+4} - \dfrac{1}{8n+5} - \dfrac{1}{8n+6}\right)$

Further references

Arndt, J. and Baenel, C. (2001) *Pi Unleashed*. New York: Springer Verlag.
Beckmann, P. (1976) *A History of Pi*. New York: St. Martin's Press.
Blatner, D. (1997) *The Joy of Pi*. New York: Walker and Co.
Borwein, J. M. and Borwein, P. B. (1987) *Pi and the AGM*. New York: Wiley.
Hardy, G. H. and Wright, E. M. (1979) *An Introduction to the Theory of Numbers*, 5th edn. Oxford: Oxford University Press (original 1938).

For more on the story of pi see:
www.projectmathematics.com/storypi

See also:
www.movie-reviews.colossus.net/movies/p/pi.html
www.cecm.sfu.ca/pi/pi

Q Quadratics and Juggling

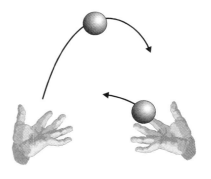

Juggling for the Complete Klutz was a Christmas present from my brother. It came with a set of 'thuds', which is what jugglers call juggling balls. As Christmas and Boxing Day rolled on I started to practise. The book is an excellent teacher and soon I was impressing everyone – well, everyone apart from the relatives who would say, 'So can you only juggle with three balls?' My response was always 'Would you like to have a try?' The author of the book talks about your friends pushing you to juggle more and more objects, and he says that this is the road to madness. I must agree with him and yet confess to starting along this road. Luckily I did not travel far, since I failed to catch many of the objects, and most of the thuds lived up to their name.

In the book the author describes how he used the idea of juggling to help in his English teaching. He was much braver than I am, and took 75 tennis balls into his classroom. I usually take six thuds and have small 'controlled' throwing chaos. You will probably discover a super student juggler in your class who will be able to demonstrate many interesting throws.

The path made by a thud is very similar to that of a standard quadratic curve, as long as you ignore air resistance. The students will clearly see the arching path of a quadratic as the thuds are thrown through the air. This gives a good practical introduction before the students put pencil to graph paper.

Experiment time

Let's look at a standard 'jug'. A jug is a three-thud juggle as shown below. The quadratics can be seen clearly. At this stage get the class to plot the quadratic $y = 10x - x^2$. If you want to be more precise, use a quadratic that exactly fits the throw. With very good groups I have used this method; otherwise the curve $y = 10x - x^2$ is as good as any other.

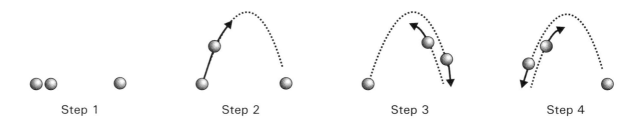

Step 1   Step 2   Step 3   Step 4

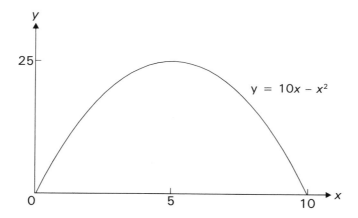

Use the rule that every x value is the same as time, so $x = 1$ is 1 second, $x = 2$ is 2 seconds, and so on. Then as the thud moves on the curve, students can plot its path for each second of the journey. By the first second it is at height 9, then after two seconds it is at height 16, and after ten it is in the right hand, as shown below.

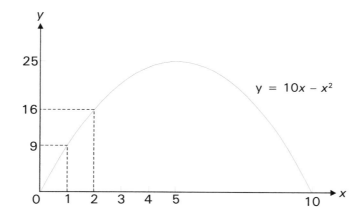

Could another thud be thrown from the right hand on the same quadratic path? No, because it would hit the descending thud from the left hand. Jugglers therefore have to move their hands. The way they do this is to move the right hand in a little and throw the second thud into the air when the first thud is at 4 seconds.

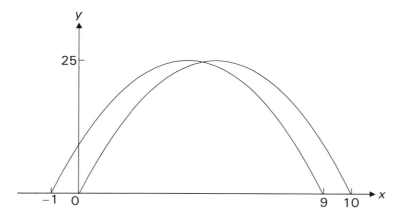

83

Using tracing paper the students will be able to construct the path of the second thud as it flies to the left hand. This equation will be a translation in the x-axis. If the student moves the graph back 1 unit along the x-axis, the equation becomes $y = 10(x + 1) - (x + 1)^2$. This equation can be checked using the graph. This verifies that each of the x-coordinates give the same values for y as the curve they have plotted using tracing paper. The second thud will then travel to the left hand, where the whole cycle is then repeated.

Give students three different-coloured counters to represent the three thuds. Then, for each second, they can move the counters along each curve to visualise what is happening. Mark each counter with a little arrow so it is easy to see the direction of motion. Remember that a second is one square in the thud's horizontal (x-axis) movement.

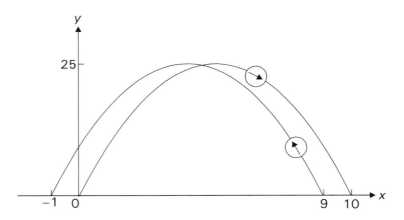

It is easy for students to get lost in the complexity of having three thuds in the air, so it is also a good idea to keep track of the movement of the thuds by constructing a table like the one shown below. This also gives the students a permanent record of the whole juggle.

Time	Thud left 1		Thud right 1		Thud left 2	
	x	y	x	y	x	y
0	0	0	10	0	0	0
1	1	9	10	0	0	0
2	2	16	10	0	0	0
3	3	21	10	0	0	0
4	4	24	9	0	0	0
5	5	25	8	9	0	0
6	6	24	7	16	0	0
7	7	21	6	21	0	0
8						
9						
10						

Students can fill in the rest of this table using their graph. Some interesting questions for them to answer are:

- Are there any other patterns that could be used for a three-thud juggle?
- Can you wait until the first thud is at $x = 5$, or $x = 6$, until you throw the second?
- In which three-thud juggles do collisions happen?

- What would happen if you start by throwing the first and second thuds from the left hand with one or two seconds' delay before you throw the third thud from the right hand? Is this a possible three-thud juggle?
- What happens when you move your hands further apart when juggling and the return thud is thrown from $x = 11$?
- Juggling with clubs requires much more space between paths to avoid collisions. Find some possible three-club juggles.

Extension ideas

We have seen how to juggle with three thuds, and juggling with four is very similar to this. So what about five? Let us first take a close look at the basic pattern before we move to the quadratic curves.

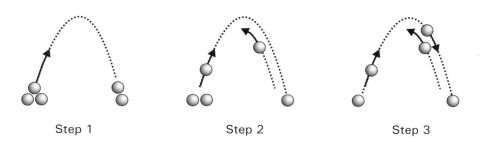

Step 1	Step 2	Step 3

Start off by holding three thuds in your left hand and two in your right. Throw one from your left hand and just before it reaches the top of the quadratic path ($x = 4$), throw one from your right hand which you have moved in to $x = 9$. Get students to check that these will not crash in mid flight.

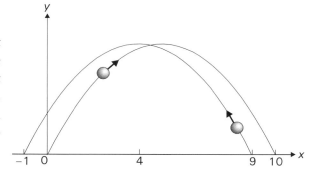

Then throw your second thud from the left hand. It should look like this.

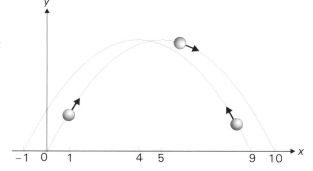

The rest is down to action and reaction. Just before a thud lands in your hand throw out the one in that hand. Always remember the jugglers' rule to move the hand towards the centre to throw, and to move the hand out to catch.

Using tracing paper to draw the curves, and counters to track the paths of the thuds as the seconds tick by, the students will be able to check for mid-air collisions.

Get students to create a table of heights (y) and horizontal distance (x) and time each of the thuds in motion, as with the three-thud juggle.

You can then try for variations on the basic throw, but be warned that the more balls in the air the greater the chance that it will all go terribly wrong! To avoid any confusion use different-coloured counters for each of the thuds used.

Further references

Cassidy, J. *et al.* (1978) *Juggling for the Complete Klutz*, 3rd edn. Palo Alto, CA: Klutz Press.

See also:
www.juggling.org/help/faqs/glossary
www.juggling.org
www.juggling.org/pics/cartoons

R Ramanujan

Srinivasa Ramanujan was one of India's greatest mathematical geniuses, yet due to his poor upbringing he did not have enough money to gain entry to an Indian University. So he wrote to Professor G. H. Hardy (see Chapter M), a great pure mathematician of the time at Cambridge University in England, asking for his help. Part of the letter that he wrote went as follows:

Srinivasa Ramanujan (1887–1920), one of India's greatest mathematical geniuses

> *After leaving school I have been employing the spare time at my disposal to work at mathematics. I have not trodden through the conventional regular course but I am striking out a new path for myself. I have found some startling results such as this formula for π which produces eight more decimal places with each term*

$$\frac{1}{2\pi\sqrt{2}} = \frac{1103}{99^2} + \left(\frac{27493}{99^6} \times \frac{1}{2} \times \frac{1\times 2}{4^2}\right) + \left(\frac{53883}{99^{10}} \times \frac{1\times 3}{2\times 4} \times \frac{1\times 3\times 5\times 7}{4^2 \times 8^2}\right) + \dots$$

Hardy studied the long list of ideas that Ramanujan had enclosed in his letter, and on the strength of them invited him to come to England to talk about them. Hardy thought that Ramanujan had a gift to be able to see mathematical solutions without working through the algebra. He stands alone in the history of mathematics as the man who could see infinity.

Experiment time

One of the areas Ramanujan worked on was infinite decimals such as cyclic decimals. The decimal equivalent of $\frac{1}{7}$ is called a cyclic decimal because the digits in the number repeat every six decimal places. For example:

$\frac{1}{7} = 0.14285714285714\dots$

$\frac{2}{7} = 0.285714285714\dots$

If you try to work out other sevenths you will see the same sort of pattern. A good question to ask is 'Why do you think that the pattern starts at a different point in each case?'

An interesting fact is that if you take the first three digits and add them to the last three, you get nines. For example, 142 + 857 = 999 and 285 + 714 = 999. This is always true for a fraction with a prime denominator if the repeating length is even.

The trouble with using a calculator to find these repeating decimals is that when you start looking at longer cycles – such as with $\frac{1}{17} = 0.058\,823\,529\,411\,764\,705\,88\ldots$ which repeats after 16 digits – you will find that your calculator only stores around 10 to 14 digits so you may think that this would be a problem. Yet there is a simple solution. By working out $\frac{2}{17}$, $\frac{3}{17}$, and so on, you will see that they all start from a different place in the cycle, so you can use these other fractions to help you work out the whole cycle.

Other good fractions for students to find the decimal equivalents for are:

$$\frac{1}{13}, \frac{1}{17}, \frac{1}{23}, \frac{1}{31}, \frac{1}{79} \text{ and } \frac{1}{891}$$

which repeat after 6, 16, 22, 15, 13 and 18 decimal places, respectively.

A general rule

A general rule for cyclic decimals is that, for a rational number, $\frac{N}{D}$, the maximum length of recurring digits will be $D - 1$. If D is prime (see Chapter M) then the length of recurring digits is a factor of $D - 1$.

For example, with $\frac{1}{13}$, which repeats after six decimals, $D - 1 = 12$, and 6 is a factor of 12.

The reverse process of finding the fraction equivalent of a decimal can also prove to be a good exercise for students. The idea is to create fractions from the cyclic decimals.

Ask the students to write down a cyclic decimal, for example 0.123 123 123 . . ., and let this be x. Then multiply this by a factor of 10, the length of the repeating part, which means multiplying by 1000 in this case. You can then find x as a fraction.

$$\begin{aligned} \text{If} \qquad x &= 0.123\,123\,123 \\ 1000x &= 123.123\,123\,123\ldots \\ 1000x &= 123 + x \\ \text{Hence} \qquad x &= \tfrac{123}{999} \end{aligned}$$

Here is another decimal example which gives a well-known fraction.

$$\begin{aligned} \text{If} \qquad x &= 0.0909\,0909\ldots \\ 100x &= 9.090\,909\,09\ldots \\ 100x &= 9 + x \\ \text{Then} \qquad x &= \tfrac{9}{99} = \tfrac{1}{11} \end{aligned}$$

Computer support

If you want to experiment with even longer decimals then you need a means of finding more digits. The computer program RAMAN prints any number of digits.

For example with the fraction $\frac{1}{891}$, correct to 20 decimal places we have

```
NUMERATOR? 1
DENOMINATOR? 891
NUMBER OF DECIMAL DIGITS REQUIRED? 20
1/891 = 0.00112233445566778900
AGAIN(Y/N)?
```

Try the following fractions – they have interesting decimals:

$$\frac{1}{81} \qquad \frac{1}{8991} \qquad \frac{1}{89991} \qquad \frac{1}{899991}$$

Can you find other fractions with interesting properties?

Further references

Hardy, G. H. (1969) *A Mathematician's Apology*. Cambridge: Cambridge University Press (originally published 1940).

Kanigel, R. (1991) *The Man Who Knew Infinity: A Life of the Genius, Ramanujan*. New York: Scribner.

Mitchell, C. (1999) *Funtastic Math! Decimals and Fractions (Grades 4–8)*. New York: Scholastic.

Olenych, B. (2000) *40 Fun-tabulous Puzzles for Multiplication, Division, Decimals, Fractions, & More*. New York: Scholastic.

See also:
www-groups.dcs.st-and.ac/~history/Mathematicians/Ramanujan.html
www.math.ufl.edu/~frank/ramanujan/things/things.html
www.ccsf.caltech.edu/~roy/upi/ramanujan.html

S Squares that are Magic

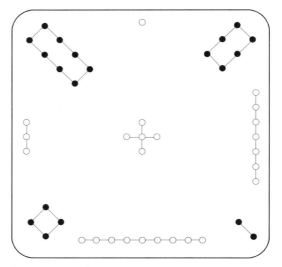

The famous Loh-Shu magic square: The Divine Turtle

A magic square is a square of numbers using the integers $1, 2, \ldots, n^2$, such that the sums of the numbers in each row, each column and each diagonal are the same. The value of these sums can be shown to be $\frac{1}{2}n\left(n^2 + 1\right)$. For example, the square above can be written

$$
\begin{array}{ccc}
8 & 1 & 6 \\
3 & 5 & 7 \\
4 & 9 & 2
\end{array}
$$

and every row, column and diagonal adds up to 15; for example $8 + 3 + 4 = 15$, $4 + 5 + 6 = 15$ and $1 + 5 + 9 = 15$. This particular magic square is also said to be a perfect magic square. The sum of any two numbers in symmetric positions with respect to the middle number are equal to twice the middle number; for example, $6 + 4 = 2 \times 5$ and $3 + 7 = 2 \times 5$.

The story goes that the first magic square ever seen was of the Divine Turtle in 2800BC. The Chinese Emperor Yu-Huang was standing watching the mighty Yellow River rush before him as the last glimmers of daylight faded from his eyes. It had been a difficult day. He had dealt with a number of problems relating to unpaid taxes, and the peasants had been revolting. As he was thinking about these problems, out on the river he saw a reflection from the newly forming night sky. It was a perfect night for star gazing for there was not a cloud to be seen. Up in the sky was a collection of stars called the Divine Turtle.

90

Emperor Yu-Huang had seen the Divine Turtle before, but tonight the pattern was so sharp that he could clearly make out all the stars. He counted carefully and recorded the pattern he saw. These numbers formed a magic square. What did this mean? He went home to bed still thinking about the problems of the day. When he woke up in the morning he remembered a dream of a turtle floating through his problems telling him how best to deal with each in turn. He proclaimed that the magic square which he had seen by the river had special powers. He commissioned an amulet to be made of the magic square. This amulet was made in gold encrusted with gemstones to symbolise the numbers one to nine. Even today people in the Far East think that these magic squares can bring good luck and ward off evil spirits.

Experiment time

The 3 × 3 magic square

A good place to start experimenting is with a 3 × 3 Divine Turtle magic square. Ask the students to find other versions of the 3 × 3 square. There are eight different versions, all of which are merely the same square, with rotations and reflections of the numbers around the central 5. You can create other special magic squares by adding the same number to each of the numbers in the square.

The 4 × 4 magic square

When you move on to 4 × 4 magic squares the possibilities grow. One example of a 4 × 4 magic square is shown here:

$$
\begin{array}{cccc}
1 & 15 & 14 & 4 \\
12 & 6 & 7 & 9 \\
8 & 10 & 11 & 5 \\
13 & 3 & 2 & 16
\end{array}
$$

The mathematician Frenicle has proved that you can find 880 magic squares using only the numbers 1 to 16.

Starting with the above magic square, ask students to find all the ways you can make a total of $34 = \frac{1}{2} \times 4 \left(4^2 + 1\right)$ with four numbers from this magic square. The different ways to do this are:

- rows, columns, and diagonals add to 34
- the four corners add to 34
- the four numbers in the centre add to 34
- the 15 and 14 in the top row and the 3 and 2 facing them in the bottom row add to 34
- the 12 and 8 in the first column and the 9 and 5 facing them in the last column add to 34
- the four squares in the corners add to 34
- if you go clockwise around the square and choose the first squares away from the corners (i.e. 15, 9, 2, 8) they add to 34.
- the same is true if you go counterclockwise.

There are other sets of four numbers that make 34, but the patterns are less striking.

If you join up the four numbers on the square that make the pattern, this will help you to visually find more relationships. You will find the following types of shapes: lines, squares, rectangles, parallelograms, and rhombuses.

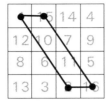 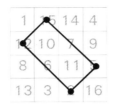 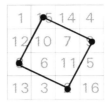

It is now becoming easier to see why people through the ages have thought that these squares have magical properties. Why should all these facts about such a simple set of numbers be true?

Here is a more general magic square, which holds true for $x > 18$:

$$
\begin{array}{cccc}
x-3 & 1 & x-6 & 8 \\
x-7 & 9 & x-4 & 2 \\
6 & x-8 & 3 & x-1 \\
4 & x-2 & 7 & x-9
\end{array}
$$

How many different magic squares can students can make from this?

Using rotations and reflections, as with 3×3 magic squares, you will be able to find some of the 880 possible squares.

Bigger magic squares

The cry from the classroom is always 'Larger, larger!' I don't know if the benefits grow as we move to 5×5 squares, 6×6 squares, and larger, but finding patterns hidden in these squares can be very rewarding for students. Here are some big magic squares:

5×5

17	24	1	8	15
23	5	7	14	16
4	6	13	20	22
10	12	19	21	3
11	8	25	2	9

6×6

1	35	4	33	32	6
25	11	9	28	8	30
24	14	18	16	17	22
13	23	19	21	20	15
12	26	27	10	29	7
36	2	34	3	5	31

7×7

30	39	48	1	10	19	28
38	47	7	9	18	27	29
46	6	8	17	26	35	37
5	14	16	25	34	36	45
13	15	24	33	42	44	4
21	23	32	41	43	3	12
22	31	40	49	2	11	20

The 8 × 8 magic square

You can create this magic square using the classic Knights Tour problem. This is a game whereby the knight moves around a chess board, landing in each square only once. Every time he lands you write a number, starting with 1 then 2, 3, 4, etc., until in the last empty square you put a 64.

I have used this with a number of groups of students of varying levels of ability, all of whom have found this task very interesting. Someone in the group usually creates the 8 × 8 knight's tour after 30–40 minutes. Ask them to explain their strategy to the rest of the class. The best strategy is to move in a circular pattern, filling in all the outside numbers and moving gradually into the centre. Once you get into the 50s it starts to get difficult to finish off the last few. I'll say no more and leave you the challenge!

To end this run of magic I would like to leave you puzzled by one of my favourite squares. It is not a standard magic square but very prime (see Chapter M). It is a consecutive prime magic square:

1480028159	1480028153	1480028201
1480028213	1480028171	1480028129
1480028141	1480028189	1480028183

There are a number of checks to be made for this one, such as are all the numbers prime and what is their sum?

Further references

Andrews, W. S. (1960) *Magic Squares and Cubes*. New York: Dover Publications (originally published 1917).

Rouse Ball, W. W. (1960) *Mathematical Recreations and Essays*, 11th edn., H. S. M. Coxeter (rev.). New York: Dover Publications (originally published 1938).

Stark, Harold M. (1978) *An Introduction to Number Theory*. Cambridge, MA: MIT Press.

See also:
www.magic-squares.com
www.grogono.com/magic/text-history.shtml

T Taylor Series in Your Calculator

There are many important discoveries made over a cup of coffee, and indirectly the scientific calculator owes its origins to a coffee house conversation. On 26 July 1712 Brook Taylor was having coffee at Child's Coffeehouse in London. Talking with another mathematician of the time he realised that a technique used by Sir Isaac Newton (see Chapter N) and another used by Dr Halley (famous for Halley's comet) were in fact particular cases of a general case. Taylor, it is said, rushed home after having coffee, to work day and night until he produced his paper on the general series that encapsulated both Newton's and Halley's work. The Taylor series formula is:

Brook Taylor (1685–1731)

$$f(a+h) = f(a) + hf^1(a) + \frac{1}{2!}h^2 f^2(a) + \frac{1}{3!}h^3 f^3(a) + \ldots$$

Taylor's infinite series was to have various uses in the future, yet the mathematical community of the time remained ignorant of its full potential for many years. It was not until 1772, when Lagrange proclaimed that Taylor's series formed the basic underlying principle of differential calculus that its importance was reconised. In 1786 the series was given the name the Taylor series, some 50 years after Taylor's death.

The same lack of recognition is also true of many of Taylor's other discoveries and much of his work was not really appreciated in his own time, possibly because his papers were difficult to follow as they were so concise. He would also touch upon general ideas in his papers but would then fail to elaborate on them fully. Mathematical historians have speculated that the reasons for all of this could have been his wealth. His family was on the fringe of nobility, so he may not have spent as much time on his mathematical hobby as someone who was working full time to earn their living. Something that we know for sure is that the scientific calculator would have had great problems in its development if it were not for his work.

Experiment time

'My calculator keeps getting things wrong!' How often do you hear this as an excuse for some error in students' calculations? Well for a certain range of numbers this statement is completely true. Calculating machines can make various types of errors: errors in the input; roundoff error; approximation error; and overflow.

- Errors in input means mistakes in typing. Typing in the wrong number will then produce an error in the final answer.
- A roundoff error is when the calculator reduces the size of your number because it does not have enough room to store the whole number exactly.
- Approximation errors occur when we use a rough guess for the number. Such as letting $\frac{1}{8} \approx 0.1$ or $\pi \approx \frac{22}{7}$.
- Overflow means that the number is too large or too small for the calculator's memory to store. If you enter 10^{100} your calculator will say it is too big, and gives the result for 10^{-100} as zero, which is clearly wrong.

Calculator accuracy

To test the accuracy of your calculator, try the following exercise. Using the cyclic decimal (see Chapter R) $\frac{1}{7} = 0.142\,857\,142\,8\ldots$ which repeats itself every six decimal places, we will be able to find out how many digits the calculator stores outside the view of the screen. The number of hidden digits plays an important role in avoiding roundoff errors, as the more digits stored, the better the calculator.

1. Enter the fraction into the calculator as $1 \div 7$. The screen shows ten decimal digits: 0.1428571429.
2. Multiply by 10 to give 1.4285714286. An extra digit which the calculator has been keeping from view has appeared on the right-hand side.
3. Subtract the first digit, in this case 1, to give 0.4285714286.
4. Multiply by 10 and subtract 4, to give 0.2857142857.
5. Multiply by 10 and subtract 2, to give 0.8571428571.
6. Multiply by 10 and subtract 8, to give 0.571428571.

Note that the final step gives no new digits on the calculator screen, so the calculator works with 13 decimal digits, showing ten, and holding a further three out of view ready to help to avoid roundoff errors. Maybe your calculator goes on to show four, five or even more hidden digits. Or maybe it did not even show three. Most modern calculators have three hidden digits. Another interesting point is to see if your calculator rounds up as the calculation is in progress. Note in step 3 the round up to . . . 6, where step 4 it gives . . . 57. This is another sign of a good calculator.

How the calculator uses the Taylor series to calculate functions

Let us take a closer look at the inner workings of a calculator. In the past students used tables to calculate functions such as sines, logarithms and square roots, which now appear on your calculator. You may think that when you push the SIN button, the calculator refers to a stored table of values and then prints out the correct result, but stop and think for a minute of all the vast range of possible numbers you could type in. A table for this range of digits would take up too much memory. So every time you press the button on the calculator for SIN, a calculation is made inside the processor. It is a very fast numerical processor so you do not even notice that this calculation is being made. For example, the calculator gives sin 50° = 0.766 044 443 1 faster than the blink of an eye. Inside the calculator the following steps occurred:

1. First, before it starts, it converts the 50 degrees into 0.872 664 626 radians. The Taylor series for sine applies for values of x in radians, so degrees have to be converted to radians using 180° = π radians.
2. Then the calculator uses the Taylor series for sine, as follows:

$$\sin x = x - \frac{1}{3!}x^3 + \frac{1}{5!}x^5 - \frac{1}{7!}x^7 + \ldots$$

With our knowledge of the sine curve this is the sort of odd function equation we might expect to get, since it is made up of a polynomial with odd indices. The exclamation mark (!) stands for factorial and is defined as $1! = 1, 2! = 1 \times 2, 3! = 1 \times 2 \times 3, 4! = 1 \times 2 \times 3 \times 4$ and so on.

Working out the first two terms gives 0.761 902 606 5, which is already close to the correct answer. If we include the x^5 term, we get 0.766 120 111 6. With the x^7 term, we get 0.766 043 639 9, which is correct to six decimal places and we have only used the first four terms of the series. Your calculator uses around 20 terms to avoid any errors in the digits it shows you.

The students can check the following series for various function values, to find the exact number of terms required to obtain one, two, three, four . . . decimal places. It is a good idea to use small values of x such as 0.1, a middle size number around 5 and something larger like 50, to see how the rate of convergence to the required number of digits changes as you change the size of the number.

- $\cos x = 1 - \frac{1}{2!}x^2 + \frac{1}{4!}x^4 - \frac{1}{6!}x^6 + \ldots$

- $\tan x = x + \frac{1}{3}x^3 + \frac{2}{15}x^5 + \frac{17}{315}x^7 + \ldots$

- $e^x = 1 + x + \frac{1}{2!}x^2 + \frac{1}{3!}x^3 + \ldots$

With the following x has to lie between −1 and +1:

- $\sin^{-1} x = x + \frac{1}{2} \times \frac{x^3}{3} + \frac{1 \times 3}{2 \times 4} \times \frac{x^5}{5} + \frac{1 \times 3 \times 5}{2 \times 4 \times 6} \times \frac{x^7}{7} + \ldots$

- $\cos^{-1} x = \frac{\pi}{2} - x - \frac{1}{2} \times \frac{x^3}{3} - \frac{1 \times 3}{2 \times 4} \times \frac{x^5}{5} - \frac{1 \times 3 \times 5}{2 \times 4 \times 6} \times \frac{x^7}{7} - \ldots$

- $\tan^{-1} x = x - \frac{1}{3}x^3 + \frac{1}{5}x^5 - \frac{1}{7}x^7 + \ldots$

- $\ln(1+x) = x - \frac{1}{2}x^2 + \frac{1}{3}x^3 - \frac{1}{4}x^4 + \ldots$

An algorithm for square root

The list above covers most of the frequently used functions on your calculator apart from the square root button. There is a powerful algorithm that can be used to find the square root of any number after only a few applications.

Let us start by trying to find the square root of two.

Choose a whole number close to the answer, say 1, and let $u_1 = 1$. Then apply the iteration formula:

$$u_{n+1} = 1 + \frac{1}{u_n + 1}$$

With $n = 1$ this gives:

$$u_2 = 1 + \frac{1}{u_1 + 1} = 1 + \frac{1}{1 + 1} = 1.5$$

With $n = 2$:

$$u_3 = 1 + \frac{1}{u_2 + 1} = 1 + \frac{1}{1.5 + 1} = 1.4$$

and so on, through $u_4 = 1.41666666$, $u_5 = 1.4137931$, $u_6 = 1.4142857$, until you converge to the correct number of decimal places required.

The same algorithm can be used for any square root with the slight modification shown below.

$$u_{n+1} = 1 + \frac{A - 1}{u_n + 1}$$

where A stands for the number you wish to find the square root of. So for $\sqrt{7}$ the iteration formula is

$$u_{n+1} = 1 + \frac{6}{u_n + 1}$$

with $u_1 = 2$, since 2 is the closest integer to the answer.

As with the Taylor series, students can use this method to find square roots and see how many applications of the algorithm are required to produce the correct number of decimal places.

Further references

Andersen, K. (1992) *Brook Taylor's Work on Linear Perspective: A Study of Taylor's Role in the History of Perspective Geometry; Including Facsimiles of Taylor's Two Books on Perspective.* New York: Springer Verlag.

Gardiner, A. (1987) *Mathematical Puzzling.* New York: Oxford University Press.

Olney, R. and Olney, P. (1977) *Pocket Calculator Fun & Games.* New York: Franklin Watts.

Pallas, N. (1976) *Calculator Puzzles, Tricks and Games.* Middletown, CT: Weekly Reader Books.

For information on calculators see:
www.webcom. com/calc
For the history of calculators see:
www.geocities.com/siliconvalley/Horizon/1404/

See also:
www-sci.lib.uci.ed/~martindale/RefCalculators.html
www.maxmon.com/1670ad

U Universes, Time Travel and Einstein

From time to time we all indulge in dreams about travelling back in time. Whenever we recall an event that happened in the past we search our memories for pictures, but wouldn't it be wonderful to actually return to that moment physically and to experience once again the happy days of childhood and heyday of youth or return to a time when we made a wrong decision? Oh, to see it all again . . .

The mystery of time travel is full of excitement. 'A wonderful adventure, but it's not science, this time travel,' I hear you say, 'and it is definitely not mathematics. Where is the proof?' Well it is out there, as they say. In 1949 Kurt Gödel, a great mathematician of the twentieth century, published solutions to Einstein's equations showing the possibility of time travel into the past. Today there are individual scientists and mathematicians all over the

Kurt Gödel (1906–1978) with Albert Einstein

world seriously studying time travel. Two of the main ones are Professor K. Thorne at the California Institute of Technology, and Professor I. Novikov at the Academy of Sciences, Astro Space Centre in Moscow. These men may not be building time machines, but they are working on Einstein's mathematical equations to gain an insight into how this could be possible. Time moves on, and what was once thought of as science fiction has, through Einstein's genius, become a possibility.

Einstein was born in 1879, and by 1905 had published his first paper which would change the way we look at the world. His paper makes a fundamental change to the way we look at light. Up until 1905 no one had thought too much about the constant speed of light. It was just another universal constant that experimental physicists attempted to calculate with greater accuracy. There was little appreciation of how radically different light waves were from sound and water waves. These sorts of waves had to travel through media such as air and water. Light did not seem to have such a medium, so one was invented for it, called the ether. The ether was thought to be all around us, yet we could not see or touch it. As with all such make-believe creations, its time was limited. The ether was only waiting for Einstein to blow it away.

No matter how you move relative to a shining light – away from or towards it – it will always look the same to you. This is not true if you think about other situations, such as cars for instance. If two cars are moving towards each other at 30 mph, it looks like 60 mph to each driver. If they are on the motorway travelling side by side at 70 mph, then it looks to each driver as if they are standing still. Light never stands still; it is always moving at $c = 299792458 \, \text{m s}^{-1}$. So how has Einstein used this idea of a constant light beam to change our view of time?

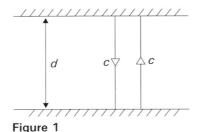

Figure 1

Let us look at this light clock. The beam of light travels back and forth between two mirrors, measuring a unit of time.

From $\text{speed} = \dfrac{\text{distance}}{\text{time}}$, $d = ct$.

If we move the clock forwards at a constant speed (v) the picture will change to the watching observer. We would see the light moving along a triangular path.

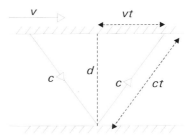

Figure 2

Using Pythagoras' theorem (see Chapter W) we can work out the following equation

$$d^2 + (vt)^2 = (ct)^2 \qquad [1]$$

Now comes the clever idea. What would we see if we were travelling with the clock? Well, to us it would just look the same as Figure 1, for we would see the clock standing still. So in terms of our time (t_1), $d = ct_1$. Using this and equation 1 gives

$$\left(ct_1\right)^2 = \left(ct\right)^2 - \left(vt\right)^2$$

$$t_1^2 = t^2\left[1 - \left(\frac{v}{c}\right)^2\right]$$

$$t_1 = t\sqrt{1 - \left(\frac{v}{c}\right)^2}$$

This is called Einstein's time dilation formula, which you can see involves no more than Pythagoras' theorem and a bit of algebra. So why did it take so long for people to discover this result? Well, it was Einstein's genius that enabled him to see aspects of the world that are not normally seen. This result also shows us that we are all time travellers. When you move your biological clock ticks slower than the biological clock of someone who is standing still!

Time slows down for you when you move: $t > t_1$. How fast do you have to travel before you notice this slowing down of time? If I go out jogging every minute of the day will I stay young? Let us look at some numbers. If, say, $t = 10$ seconds for someone standing still, how much time would pass if you moved at a speed of $v = 2\,000\,000 \, \text{m s}^{-1}$. Using the time dilation formula gives $t_1 = 9.9777$ for the moving person. You may think that this difference is small, but over a year this would amount to around eight extra days, and over a lifetime an extra two years! But as always there is a catch, and you may have already spotted it. What sort of machine can get to speeds of two million metres per second? At present nothing can, but who knows what the future holds?

Students will enjoy calculating the time they save as they go faster. The following gives you some values to work on for $t = 10\,000$ seconds:

Speed (m s^{-1})	Time for the traveller t_1 (s)
10 000	9 999.9999
100 000	9 999.9988
1 000 000	9 999.8888
10 000 000	9 994.4352
100 000 000	9 427.2742
200 000 000	7 449.4293
250 000 000	5 519.0009
290 000 000	2 534.9813

The change in time as we get close to the speed of light in the last value gives three-quarters more time to the moving person. By the time the person standing still is 100 years old, the moving one would be only 25. Do you think this means that businessmen who are continually on aeroplanes travelling around the world will age less?

Experiment time

There is another side to how Einstein made us think. What is the shape of space? What shape could our universe be? Centuries ago, people believed that the Earth was flat and they would fall off the edge if they went too far. Today we know that it is a sphere which you can travel around for ever and eventually come back to where you started. Could the universe be like this? Just a very, very big sphere, cylinder or doughnut? It is a question for which we do not yet have answers. Some people think that the stars we see in the sky may just be the light that left our own Sun billions of years ago, having travelled around the universe and come back to us.

Using some well-known shapes and games you can get students to experiment with space and shape.

Take a cylinder. If you unwrap it, it becomes a rectangle. The arrows on the sides show the sides to join to get the original shape.

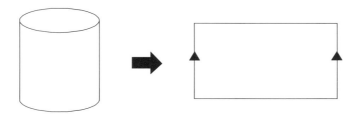

Starting with a rectangle, by joining one pair of sides we get a cylinder. Then join the ends of the cylinder to get a doughnut, or torus.

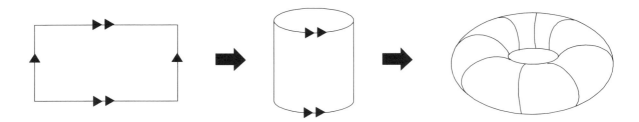

A good game to play with this doughnut shape is noughts and crosses. To start with, play the game a few times on a normal board. Then develop the idea into your doughnut surface. The possibilities for three in a row are greatly increased, and the students will find a number of strategies to win. The game shown here is won by crosses, as they have three in a row.

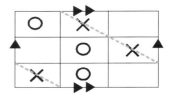

I have played other board games on a doughnut. The choice of games is only limited by your resources. The students gain great spatial awareness in what to them is just a fun game. I often find students playing these games in breaktime after I have covered them during the lesson.

Extension ideas

How to build a time machine!

I don't know about you, but I always feel somewhat cheated when I read about time machines. I'm told all these facts and yet no one tells me how to build one! So as not to cheat you, here is the humble time machine with great thanks to Professor Tipler. Professor Tipler published a paper on how to build a time machine back in 1976. This machine would enable you to go back in time.

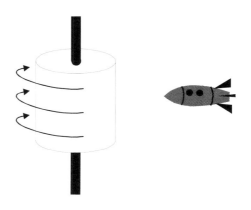

First, with increased funding from your LEA, you need to buy a large cylinder, and when I say large, I mean large. This cylinder needs to be the mass of the the Sun, but very densely packed together. Start it rotating faster and faster, until it is rotating so fast that it starts to disturb the fabric of both space and time around it.

Then get into your fast vehicle. It needs to be fast if you want to get back to the future, if you consider the time dilation we discussed at the beginning of this chapter. Start to approach the spinning cylinder, and as you get closer strange things will start to happen. Your path, which normally inextricably moves you forward in time, changes, since moving around the cylinder in the direction of rotation moves you back in time. As the direction of time is collapsed into the past, what strange things do you see in this distorted moment of space time? Moving away from the rotating cylinder sets the direction of time back to normal for you, but now you are in the past . . .

Further references

Bondi, J. (1980) *Relativity and Common Sense: A New Approach to Einstein*. New York: Dover (originally published 1964).

Gribbin, J. (1995) *In Search of the Edge of Time*. Harmondsworth: Penguin.

Lightman, A. (1994) *Einstein's Dreams*. London: Bloomsbury.

Nahin, P. J. (1993) *Time Machines: Time Travel in Physics, Metaphysics, and Science Fiction*. New York: American Institute of Physics.

Novikov, I. D. (1988) *The River of Time*, V. Kisin (trans.). Cambridge: Cambridge University Press.

Stannard, R. and Levers, J. (1989) *The Time and Space of Uncle Albert*. London: Faber.

Thorne, K. S. (1994) *Black Holes and Time Warps: Einstein's Outrageous Legacy*. London: Picador.

Tipler, F. J. (1974) 'Rotating Cylinders and the Possibility of Global Causality Violations', *Physical Review D*, **9**(8), 2203–6

Tipler, F. J. (1994) *The Physics of Immortality: Modern Cosmology, God and the Resurrection of the Dead*. Basingstoke: Macmillan.

For the shape of space see www.geom.umn.edu/locate/sos/

See also:
www.netlabs.net/hp/tremor/wormholes.html
www.time.com/time/time100/poc/magazine/albert_einstein5a
www.time-travel.com

V Von Neumann and Computers

The title of this chapter should not be Von Neumann and computers, but Von Neumann and the Von Neumann machine. Von Neumann may be famous for many things but humility was not one of them. Yet no one had anything bad to say about 'good time' Johnny Von Neumann; he just was too likeable. He gave massive parties and loved women, fast cars, jokes, noise, Mexican food, fine wine, and, most of all, mathematics. 'Unbelievable', said one of Von Neumann's old friends, 'He knew how to have a good time. His parties were once if not twice a week at 26 Wetcott Road. Waiters came around with drinks all night long. Dancing and loud laughter. With Von Neumann at the centre of it all, he was a fantastically witty man.'

Johnny von Neumann (1903– 1957)

In a way Von Neumann could afford to party, since he had been born lucky – lucky enough to have a great mind, that did not forget. He had a true photographic memory and never forgot a thing. The story goes that you could ask him to quote from anything he had ever read, and the only question he would ask you was, 'When do you want me to stop?' In addition to having a great memory, he was also very fast. Start asking him a question and, before you finished, he would be answering, and suggesting interesting follow-ups that you should consider. It's no wonder, with a super mind like his, that he is credited with inventing the present-day computer.

When one of the first computers was to be tested, Von Neumann was on hand to help. The test for the computer was to work out powers of 2, and to find the first number to have 7 as its fourth digit from the right. The computer and Von Neumann started at the same time, and you guessed it, Johnny finished first!

As well as working on the development of the computer, Von Neumann also worked on the atom bomb and created a branch of mathematics called game theory. His work in these areas argued strategies for the Cold War and inspired the movies *Dr Strangelove* and *War Games*.

When Von Neumann finished building his computer he had to find a use for it. In his eyes the only useful thing to do was mathematics so he and fellow mathematicans Fermi and Ulam invented a simulation method that they called the Monte Carlo method. This method simulates random events using the computer. In Buffon's needle problem (see Chapter B) the JAVA applet uses Von Neumann's simulation method to validate the correct value of pi. To simulate the unpredictable event of throwing a needle, the computer has to use something called a pseudo-random number generator. The pattern of numbers generated are deterministic, yet of sufficient complexity to cause the outcome to appear unpredictable (random). In the following experiments we will look in more detail at random number generators.

Experiment time

There is a problem in mathematics called the random walk. You start with a player at some point. He tosses a coin, and how it falls decides his direction of motion. This randomly makes the choice of which way to go.

To set the scene for students, imagine that you are on a narrow mountain ridge. It is windy and the rain is battering down on you. This makes it difficult to see where you are going. Every time you move forward you get blown randomly to the left or right. What are your chances of making it across the ridge?

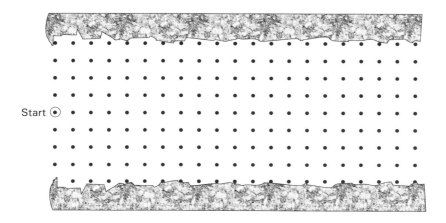

Start at the base camp dot, and throw a coin. If it is heads move to the right and if it is tails move to the left. For example, if you throw HHTHTTH then it would look like this:

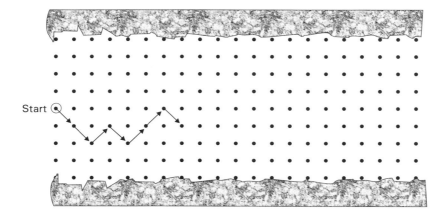

Keep throwing the coin until you make it to the other side or fall off the edge.

What is the chance that you will:

- fall off the cliff
- make it to the other side
- fall off before the tenth move
- fall off before the fifteenth move
- fall off the right or left side of the ridge?

Before you start this experiment using paper, it is a good idea to let the students try to walk the ridge for 'real' in the classroom. With a pre-defined ridge marked on the floor, you can flip the coin to say move left or right. This works well as a starter to get them thinking about how wide the ridge needs to be if they are to make it to the other side. After this introduction get students to perform this experiment on paper at least five times, then collect the data on the board. Be as detailed in this collection phase as the class's ability allows. For example, you may ask if anyone went over the edge in the first 5 moves, or between 6 and 10 moves, or 11 and 15 moves, and so on. Once you have collected the results the class can then talk about the probability of crossing the ridge.

Here are some extension ideas for this task:

- Instead of using a coin use the random number button (RAN#) on your calculator, moving to the right if the number generated is in the range 0–0.5, and to the left for higher numbers.
- What happens if the wind blows harder from one side? Does this make it more difficult to cross the ridge? Simulate this by moving to the right for random numbers 0–0.3, and to the left otherwise, or something similar.
- Include the chance that you will be blown two dots to the right or left.

Using mathematics to predict this random event

One question you can ask is how far on average the ridge walker will move away from the centre line after the start. Let the centre line be the x-axis. If you move to the left this is +1, and if you move to the right this is –1.

Let D_n be the distance from the centre line after n steps. This can be found from D_{n-1}, and since to get to the next step you would have to add or subtract one to the previous step, $D_n = D_{n-1} + 1$ or $D_n = D_{n-1} - 1$. If you then square these equations you obtain

$$D_n^2 = \begin{cases} D_{n-1}^2 + 2D_{n-1} + 1 \\ D_{n-1}^2 - 2D_{n-1} + 1 \end{cases}$$

Adding these two equations together,

$$D_n^2 = D_{n-1}^2 + 1 \qquad [1]$$

After one step, $D_1^2 = 1$. Using this, and equation 1 repeatedly, we can obtain $D_n^2 = n$. Therefore $D_n = \sqrt{n}$. This tells us that, on average, after n steps you would have moved $\sqrt{n}$ away from the centre line.

Calculating the probabilities

To calculate the probabilities involved in the random walk, you can use Pascal's triangle (see Chapter G) to get the chances of following different routes in a random path, for at each step you are making a decision to go left or right. The numbers in the triangle indicate the number of routes from the start position to that point. To find the next line in Pascal's triangle add together the two roots to that point.

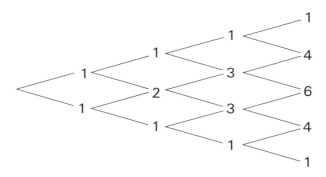

Extension ideas

- The 147 random number generator works in the following way. First it selects a decimal between 0 and 1, which it then multiples by 147. Then it takes the fractional part of this result and multiplies it by 10. The integer it produces is the random number.

  For example, if the decimal between 0 and 1 that is selected is 0.1357, we have

    $0.1357 \times 147 = 19.9479$

  The fractional part is 0.9479

    $10 \times 0.9497 = 9.479$

  So the random number is 9.

  If you want a larger random number using this method, just multiply by 100 or 1000 in the final stage. Try finding some random numbers using the program RAN147.

  A good challenge for the students is to discover when the random generator is not working efficiently. In other words, when you can spot a pattern in the numbers. To make it easier for the students, tell them to use a single-digit decimal, such as 0.7, at first, and build up to two digits and more. Be warned, the time for the pattern to repeat will grow very quickly as you increase the digits.

  This type of generator is the simplest. After a number of random numbers you will see a pattern as the sequence of decimals is calculated. In the example above, starting with a four-digit number such as 0.1357, after 10 000 numbers or fewer we will get a repeat.

- Add the random numbers generated from your calculator's random button until their total exceeds 1. Note how many numbers are required. You will find that the average number of random numbers required is e = 2.7182818 . . . (see Chapter E). Changing the total to 3, so that the average becomes 8, makes a good challenge for students.

- A similar idea is to find the average random number between 0 and 1. This is a problem that the students can work on using their calculators by finding the average of blocks of ten numbers. The answer comes to

$$\int_0^1 x \, dx = \tfrac{1}{2}$$

In other words, this is the area under the curve $y = x$ from $x = 0$ to 1. What about the average of random numbers squared, or cubed . . .?

Further references

Aspray, W. (1990) *John von Neumann and the Origins of Modern Computing*. Cambridge, MA: MIT Press.

Berg, H. C. (1993) *Random Walks in Biology*. Princeton, NJ: Princeton University Press.

Dyson, F. J. (1981) *Disturbing the Universe*. London: Pan.

Gentle, J. E. (1998) *Random Number Generation and Monte Carlo Methods*. New York and London: Springer.

Malkiel, B. G. (1985) *A Random Walk down Wall Street*. New York: Norton.

Spitzer, F. (1964) *Principles of Random Walk*. Princeton, NJ: Van Nostrand.

Von Neumann, J. (2000) *The Computer and the Brain*, 2nd edn. New Haven, CT and London: Yale Nota Bene.

For a number of random walk movies see http://cic.nist.gov/lipman/sciviz/random

See also:
www.math.uah.edu/Stat/walk/
http://math.furman.edu/~dcs/java/rw
http://polymer.bu.edu/java/
www.random.org/essay.html

For a computer simulation of a random walk along a line see:
www.math.sc.edu/~sumner/RandomWalk.html
Here is a screen shot from it.

Number of Trials	10
Start At	4
Path Length	7

Walk: - - - + - - -

Steps in this walk: 13

After 5 walks the average number of steps is 6.2   Ex2 is 42.6

Theoretical Average number of steps is 9

GO   STOP   RESET

W Wolfskehl, Wiles, Pythagoras and Diophantus

Paul Wolfskehl was professor of mathematics in Darmstadt in Germany in the early 1900s. He spent many long hours attempting in vain to prove one of the greatest unsolved problems in mathematics – Fermat's last theorem.

Fermat's last theorem is the claim by Pierre de Fermat in the 1650s that there are no positive integers (see Chapter I) x, y and z such that, for $n > 2$, $x^n + y^n = z^n$. Note that if $n = 2$ then $x^2 + y^2 = z^2$ is the well-known Pythagoras' theorem for which we can find many integer solutions, such as $3^2 + 4^2 = 5^2$ and $5^2 + 12^2 = 13^2$. More about this later in the chapter.

As well as being unable to solve his maths problem, Wolfskehl was also disappointed in love, so he decided to end his life. Being a methodical man he wrote a suicide note specifying the date and hour that he would commit the act. Within a few hours of the appointed time, he decided to occupy his final hours with one last try at Fermat's problem. He became so engrossed that the time passed quickly and he forgot all about suicide. Several

Pierre de Fermat (1601–1665)

hours later, still unable to solve the problem, he decided to begin life again with renewed vigour, and tore up the suicide note. You could say that mathematics saves lives. When Wolfskehl finally died many years later through natural causes he left 100,000 marks in his will to the first person to prove Fermat's last theorem.

It took nearly 100 years for this prize to be claimed, and the solution has become one of the greatest in mathematical history. Andrew Wiles said, on finding the solution,

> *suddenly, totally unexpectedly, I had this incredible revelation. It was the most important moment of my working life. Nothing I ever do again . . . it was so indescribably beautiful, it was so simple and so elegant, and I just stared in disbelief for twenty minutes, then during the day I walked round and round in a daze coming back to my desk to see if it was still there . . .*

He says it is simple, yet the proof fills hundreds of pages with highly complex algebra that only a few people in the world can understand. Wiles created the proof in 1994, demonstrating that real mathematics is going on now and not just long ago in the distant past. Wiles also says that he first met this problem at the age of 10, and even then he remembers thinking what a beautiful problem it was. Mathematicians call a problem beautiful if it is easy to state yet hard to solve.

The special case when $x^2 + y^2 = z^2$ can be solved, and has become one of the most well-known formulas in mathematics. Pythagoras lived around 500BC and, owing to his theorem, is one of the most well-known mathematicians who has ever lived. He formed a school on the Greek Island of Samos. Students of the school were called Pythagoreans and had a strict code of beliefs almost like school rules. They believed that:

- at its deepest level, reality is mathematical in nature;
- philosophy can be used for spiritual purification;
- the soul can rise to union with the divine;
- certain symbols have a mystical significance;
- all brothers of the order should observe strict loyalty and secrecy.

Pythagoras (569BC–475BC), who is credited with the theorem $x^2 + y^2 = z^2$, although the result was known to the Babylonians 1200 years earlier

When Pythagoras discovered his famous theorem he slaughtered 100 oxen to thank the gods for the inspiration. Babylonian tablets containing extensive lists of Pythagorean triples have been found dating from 1700BC, so we can see that history does not always credit the right person!

Experiment time

A good experiment for students is to work out other Pythagorean triples, which are sets of three numbers, such as 3, 4, 5, satisfying $x^2 + y^2 = z^2$. You can give them the longest side, z, and ask them to find the two squares that satisfy the equation.

This is difficult without a good starting point, so the following trial and improvement method will help.

- **Step 1:** Using millimetre-squared paper draw the longest side at an angle so that the ends are approximately close to whole squares on the paper. Then form a right-angled triangle. For example, if $z = 17$ we could draw it like this.

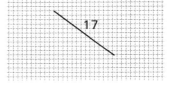

- **Step 2:** From the line drawn on squared paper, take approximate integer values for x and y. Approximate values with the line drawn at this angle are about 10 and 14.

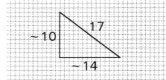

- **Step 3:** Check these numbers with Pythagoras' formula

$$17^2 = 289$$
$$14^2 + 10^2 = 296$$

So these numbers aren't right, but they are close!

- **Step 4:** Use trial and improvement to obtain the correct answer. Change 14^2 to 15^2:

$$17^2 - 15^2 = 289 - 225 = 64 = 8^2$$

So $x = 8$, $y = 15$, $z = 17$, and the Pythagorean triple is 8, 15, 17.

After a few minutes the students will have found lots of triples. I usually write them on the board as the students find them. Then, quite independently, the students will split into two types: those who like to check to see if the results on the board are correct, and those who want to find more.

Here are some more triples:

x	3	5	7	8	9	11	12	13	16
y	4	12	24	15	40	60	35	84	63
z	5	13	25	17	41	61	37	85	65

Questions you may hear are 'How many triples can you find?', 'What's the largest one you've found?', 'Sir, what is the maximum number of triples that you can find?' An efficient method of producing triples is by using the identity:

$$(2mn)^2 + (m^2 - n^2)^2 = (m^2 + n^2)^2, \text{ with } m > n$$

It can be proved that all Pythagorean triples are of this form. So by taking values for m and n you can find all triples. For example, with $m = 3$ and $n = 2$ we have

$$(2 \times 3 \times 2)^2 + (3^2 - 2^2)^2 = (3^2 + 2^2)^2$$
$$12^2 + 5^2 = 13^2$$

So the Pythagorean triple is 5, 12, 13. You can use this identity to find all triples with corresponding values of m and n.

Computer support

The computer program PYTHAGOR allows you to find all the triples up to a certain value for m. The example run shown in the screen shot is for triples up to $m = 7$ and $n = 6$.

```
TRIPLES UP TO? 7
M= 2   N= 1      4           3           5
M= 3   N= 1      6           8          10
M= 3   N= 2     12           5          13
M= 4   N= 1      8          15          17
M= 4   N= 2     16          12          20
M= 4   N= 3     24           7          25
M= 5   N= 1     10          24          26
M= 5   N= 2     20          21          29
M= 5   N= 3     30          16          34
M= 5   N= 4     40           9          41
M= 6   N= 1     12          35          37
M= 6   N= 2     24          32          40
M= 6   N= 3     36          27          45
M= 6   N= 4     48          20          52
M= 6   N= 5     60          11          61
M= 7   N= 1     14          48          50
M= 7   N= 2     28          45          53
M= 7   N= 3     42          40          58
M= 7   N= 4     56          33          65
M= 7   N= 5     70          24          74
M= 7   N= 6     84          13          85
AGAIN(Y/N)?
```

Extension ideas

- For any positive integer n, show that $2n$, $n^2 - 1$, $n^2 + 1$ is a Pythagorean triple. What pattern links the hypotenuse and one of the other sides in this type of triangle?

- If a, b, c and x, y, z are Pythagorean triples, show that $ax - by, ay + bx, cz$ is a Pythagorean triple.

- The equation $x^2 + y^2 = z^2$ is also an example of a Diophantus' equation. Diophantus' equations are those that have integer solutions. The Greek mathematician Diophantus of Alexandria lived around AD250. He published 13 books on the algebra of equations with integer solutions, six of which have been preserved. He was one of the first mathematicians to use a type of algebraic notation in his equations when he was searching for these integer solutions.

  Students who find Pythagorean triples interesting may want to work on the equation $x^2 + y^2 = 5z^2$, which is another type of Diophantus' equation. Some of its solutions are:

x	2	4	6	8	11
y	1	2	3	4	2
z	1	2	3	4	5

  The general form of this equation is

  $$(m^2 + 4mn - n^2)^2 + (2m^2 - 2mn - 2n^2)^2 = (m^2 + n^2)^2$$

  with m and n greater than zero. Notice that this is similar to the identity for Pythagoras' equation. The program DIOPHAN finds all the triples for this equation.

- Diophantus' tomb has the epitaph:

  > This tomb holds Diophantus. Ah, how great a marvel!
  > The tomb tells scientifically the measure of his life.
  > God granted him to be a boy for the sixth part of his life,
  > and adding a twelfth part to this,
  > he clothed his cheeks with down;
  > he lit him the light of wedlock after a seventh part,
  > and five years after his marriage he granted him a son.
  > Alas! Late-born wretched child;
  > after attaining the measure of half his father's life,
  > chill fate took him. After consoling his grief by this science
  > of numbers for four years he ended his life.

  So how old was Diophantus when he died?

Further references

Heath, T. L. (1964) *Diophantus of Alexandria: A Study in the History of Greek Algebra*, 2nd edn. New York: Dover Publications.

Iamblichus (1986) *Life of Pythagoras, or, Pythagoric Life: Accompanied by Fragments of the Ethical Writings of Certain Pythagoreans in the Doric Dialect and a Collection of Pythagoric Sentences from Stobaeus and Others*, T. Taylor (trans.). Rochester, VT. : Inner Traditions International.

See also:
www.geocities.com/capecanaveral/launchpad/3740/
www.pbs.org/wgbh/nova/proof/puzzle/theorem
www.aboutscotland.com/harmony/prop
www.mathsoft.com/asolve

X X,Y,Z Coordinates, Descartes and Tennis Balls

René Descartes is famous for his philosophical saying, 'I think, therefore I am', yet he was, as many clever men of the seventeenth century were, a great all-rounder. His intellectual skills also encompassed mathematics and, in particular, geometry. In 1636 he published his work on algebraic methods for geometry. He used the x-, y-, z-coordinate frame he had created as a foundation on which algebraic geometry could be used. The coordinate system based on the x-, y-, z-axis system is called, after him, the Cartesian coordinate system. The idea came to him while lying ill in bed. 'I saw a fly climbing the wall and thought – How can I specify the fly's location unambiguously in such a way that others can understand me?'

The French mathematician and philosopher René Descartes (1596–1650)

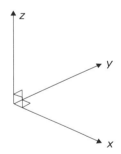

Algebraic geometry has many benefits, as we will see later in this chapter. It will help us in the analysis of the motion of a ball, as we can use the non-linear algebraic equations of the ball's flight path to plot the graph of the ball as it travels through the air. These equations can then be solved using experimental data. It would not be possible to find the drag and lift factors without this interplay between algebra and geometry.

As with all people with great minds, Descartes knew his place in the history of mathematics and left us with this quote, which shows his obvious love of puzzling things out.

I hope that posterity will judge me kindly, not only as to the things which I have explained, but also to those which I have intentionally omitted so as to leave others the pleasure of discovery.

114

Experiment time

A sunny day in July, when the exams are over and your students still have Wimbledon memories, is a good time to confront, head on, the resisting medium called air. This resistance is noticeable in your classroom, or if you wish to go outside you will find it, as long as the wind does not blow your results away.

The first thing to do is to organise your class into groups of four students. Each group will require:

- a stop watch
- a long ruler
- a protractor
- a tennis ball

If you want to do the experiment with a different type of ball this is fine. You will find that different types of balls have their own unique values of drag, since the air causes drag in different ways on various surfaces. The size of the ball, the shape of the front facing edge and weight are also important, since the larger these quantities are, in general, the slower the ball will move through the air.

The experiment involves throwing a tennis ball to another student to catch. During its journey the students will measure how long this takes and how high the ball goes. From this they will be able to find the drag factor of the ball. During the experiment, the thrower of the ball plays a key role. They should try to throw the ball at the same measured angle and speed for each throw, to maintain consistency in the data being collected by the other students. At one school in which I worked we were lucky enough to have a tennis ball launcher. This creates regularity in the ball's initial speed and direction, thus eliminating any irregularities that the thrower may cause.

When carrying out the experiment you will need to collect the following data:

- time to travel from A to D
- angle to the horizontal, θ
- maximum height, *BC*
- horizontal distance to maximum height, *AB*

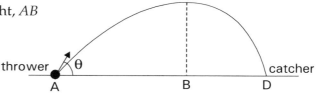

The experiment should be performed several times until the students have consistent data. One problem you may encounter is trying to find the maximum height. A good idea is to use a long pole, marking on it the approximate position of C. Then during the experiment observe to see if C should be higher or lower. Repeating this procedure you can close in on the exact value of the maximum height.

Once all the data have been collected you are ready to analyse it. The program overleaf is written for a Casio graphics calculator and is available on the CD-ROM in a file called GTENNIS, which you can use as a download for your calculator. It is useful to use graphics calculators if you are experimenting outside as the students can find one value of drag, then try throwing the ball higher or faster to see if they get the same value for drag. If you perform the experiment inside then you may prefer to use the BASIC program called TENNIS, which is included in computer support.

Calculator program

Initialise variables $0{\rightarrow}X : 0{\rightarrow}Y : 0.1{\rightarrow}H :$

Inputs   "V"?$\rightarrow$V : "Q"?$\rightarrow$Q :
"D"?$\rightarrow$D : "L"?$\rightarrow$L :

Set up at mid interval   VcosQ$\rightarrow$M : VsinQ$\rightarrow$N :
$-V^2$(DcosQ + LsinQ)$\rightarrow$A : $-9.8+V^2$(LcosQ – DsinQ)$\rightarrow$B :
M + 0.05A$\rightarrow$M : N + 0.05B$\rightarrow$N :

Main program   LBI 1 : X+HM$\rightarrow$X : Y+HN$\rightarrow$Y :
$\sqrt{N^2 + M^2}$ $\rightarrow$V : $\tan^{-1}$(N÷M)$\rightarrow$Q :
$-V^2$(DcosQ + LsinQ)$\rightarrow$A : $-9.8 + V^2$(LcosQ – DsinQ)$\rightarrow$B :
M + HA$\rightarrow$M : N + HB$\rightarrow$N :
PLOT X,Y :

Printout results $Y < 0 \Rightarrow X$
$Y < 0 \Rightarrow T$
H + T$\rightarrow$T : GOTO 1

When the program is running the calculator will ask for the initial speed and the angle of elevation. An approximate value for the initial speed can be found from

$$v = \frac{AD}{\text{time} \times \cos\theta}$$

The values for drag and lift (D and L) are obtained by trial and error until the predictions from the model agree with the measurements from the experiment. Only drag is required when looking at the basic tennis ball model, so enter 0 for the lift. (Later on, in the extension ideas, I will talk about how lift can be used.) The program will plot the path of the tennis ball and give the:

- distance travelled in the X-direction when $Y = 0$
- time to travel this distance.

Adjust the RANGE to fit AD (given X_{min} and X_{max}) and BC (Y_{min} and Y_{max}) then modify your guess for drag (D) until you obtain a good fit within this box. With the program TENNIS you can do the same thing by adjusting line

```
10   WINDOW(0,0)-(40,20)
```

With a little practice you will be able to find the drag factor of any ball in no time at all. The drag factor is the air resistance caused by the ball as it travels through the air. I am always pleased at how quick students find these drag factors. I think this is due to the fact that they are only changing one variable slightly and seeing an instant effect on the screen. Using a light ball the drag is much more noticeable than you would ever imagine.

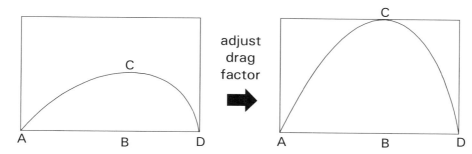

Adjust the drag factor until the curve fits exactly in the range given by *AD* (X) and *BC*(Y)

Extension ideas

The same experiment can be performed with a Frisbee, but it is advisable to increase the number of reference points, using not just C, as with the tennis ball. I have found that three reference points are usually sufficient. Then by trial and error you can find the drag (D) and lift (L). Performing this experiment indoors reduces other external factors on the Frisbee, such as wind. School corridors are also very good experimental areas for Frisbees!

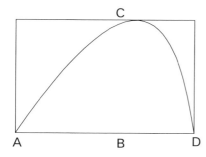

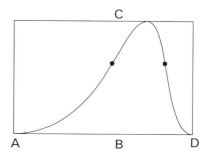

When you throw a tennis ball and it is affected by drag, you will get pictures like this.

With a Frisbee you get drag and lift, so the curve is different. The points shown indicate the other points of reference.

Another extension idea is to use the computer program to find drag and lift factors which will give world record distances such as the ones shown in the table.

Projectile	Maximum distance (m)
Flying ring	395.63
Boomerang (non-returning)	200.00 (unofficial)
Frisbee	167.84
Boomerang (returning)	146.00 (flightpath > 450m)
Baseball throw	135.88
Cricket throw	128.60
Javelin	94.58
Football kick	91.00
Hammer throw	79.30
Discus	70.86
Shot-put	22.00

Further references

Daish, C. B. (1972) *The Physics of Ball Games*. London: English Universities Press.

De Mestre, N. (1990) *The Mathematics of Projectiles in Sport*. Cambridge: Cambridge University Press.

Kooy, J. M. J. (1950) *Ballistics of the Future*. Russia.

Walker, J. (1975) *The Flying Circus of Physics*. New York: Wiley.

Watts, R. G. and Bahill, A. T. (2000) *Keep your Eye on the Ball, the Science and Folklore of Baseball*, 2nd edn. New York W. H. Freeman.

For general Frisbee information see www.ira.uka.de/~thgries/disc/

For the US Boomerang Association see www.usba.org

See also www.frisbee.com

Y Yo-yos, Superballs and Other Toys

We all played with yo-yos, superballs, spinning tops and other such toys when we were young. These types of toys are part of childhood and I find that students feel happy to experiment with them. I use them to help improve algebra skills. You will also find that, within a group of students, there will be experts in one or more of these toys. Someone will know how to 'walk the dog' or 'spin a back flip', or will know more about gyroscopes than you do. This always adds to these lessons, for I simply hand over the toy and say, 'Show me what you can do'. Sometimes when you are a teacher you have to just sit back and say 'Gosh, that's clever' to your students.

Experiment time

Yo-yo

Why does a yo-yo come back up the string when it has been cast downwards from the hand? To answer this question we need to look at the yo-yo's motion in detail. When the yo-yo has reached the lowest point in its motion, it spins in a small loop at the end of the string. The reason for this spinning is due to the light contact made between the string and the yo-yo. Giving the string a sudden movement upwards greatly increases the contact force between the yo-yo and the string. The yo-yo will then stop sliding and start to wrap itself up the string. This is the basic mechanics of its motion.

A good trick to start the lesson is to send the yo-yo to 'sleep'. In other words, send it down the string fast, so it just sits spinning at the bottom of the string. Then take the string off your finger and hold it in your hand. Slap the back of this hand and watch the yo-yo start to climb. As soon as you see it climbing back up the string, let go of the string. The yo-yo will continue upwards. When it has wound itself up, catch it. This creates a good moment to introduce algebra.

Assuming that it starts from rest, the equation of motion of a yo-yo is:

$$gx = \tfrac{1}{2}v^2 + \tfrac{1}{4}R^2\omega^2$$

where v is the speed of the yo-yo, ω is the speed of spin measured in radians per second, r is the inner radius (usually $0.01\,$m), R is the outer radius (usually $0.03\,$m), g is the gravitational constant (approximately $10\,$m$\,$s^{-2}) and x is the vertical downwards distance travelled.

Questions

1. Rewrite the equation so v^2 is the subject.
2. Rewrite the equation so ω^2 is the subject.
3. Given that $v = r\omega$, write the equation from question 1 with no ω's.
4. Using the above numbers, and taking the length of the string to be $1.4\,$m, or using your own yo-yo's specifications, find the speed of the yo-yo when it reaches the bottom of the string.
5. So far we have assumed that the yo-yo has no speed at the start. If we assume that the speed at the start is u, the equation becomes

$$\tfrac{1}{2}u^2 + gx = \tfrac{1}{2}v^2 + \tfrac{1}{4}R^2\omega^2 .$$

   Does the extra speed at the start make much difference?
6. Repeat questions 1 to 4 with the new equation in question 5.

Superball

Originally made by Wham-O in 1970, superballs are now produced by a number of manufacturers. They are made from very elastic rubber, so when they are dropped they bounce very well.

First, take a large and small superball and stick them together with a piece of Blu-tack. When these balls are dropped to the ground, the small ball has a maximum possible rebound of nearly nine times its original height. A good experiment is to measure the drop and the rebound heights. I have always found that a small drop will produce the best results, since there is less interference from the air. Please note that when you are performing this experiment, the smaller superball will fly off when it hits the ground, so you need to take care.

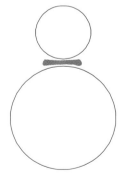

The algebra to obtain the nine times original height result

Given that at the moment of impact the balls have speed v, then after the collision the smaller ball will have speed $3v$. Using this information and the equation $(\text{speed})^2 = 2g \times \text{height}$, you can show the nine times relation.

Why 3v?

The $3v$ comes from the two equations

$$2v = v_1 - v_2$$

$$m_2v - m_1v = m_1v_1 + m_2v_2$$

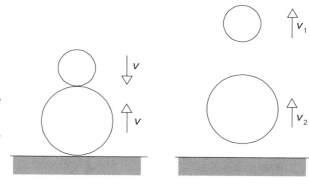

where m_1 and m_2 are the masses of the smaller and larger balls respectively.

Solving these equations to find the speed v_1 of the smaller ball gives

$$v_1 = \frac{3m_2v - m_1v}{m_1 + m_2}$$

This implies that when m_1 is very small compared to m_2, v_1 is $3v$. This is why you need to use a large and a small superball, since the most important factor for a high bounce is the relative difference in the weights of the balls.

Extension ideas

1. Use a ping-pong ball instead of the small superball, since it is much lighter and so will gain more height.
2. There is a critical mass ratio of 3:1. This guarantees that the heavier ball will stay on the floor, and the lighter will have twice the speed after impact than before impact. This causes it to reach four times its initial height.

Gyroscope

A spinning top, which we all played with as children, is a type of gyroscope. Set a top spinning on the floor and watch its motion. You will observe that as its spin gradually slows down it begins to precess. This means that its stem or spin axis will rotate around a vertical axis. This motion is caused by its weight pulling it down to the ground.

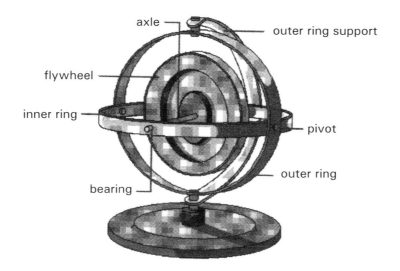

The equation governing the speed of precession, v, and speed of spin, ω, is:

$$v = \frac{gbc}{\omega a}$$

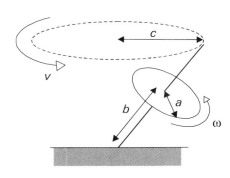

where a is the radius of the gyroscope, b the distance to the centre, c the distance to the centre of precession and g is the gravitational constant (take its value to be $10\,\mathrm{m\,s^{-2}}$).

You can buy small gyroscopes from most toy shops. A gyroscope has a disc that spins around a central stem axis. These are much better for demonstration use than one of the standard children's spinning tops, as they will spin for a much longer period of time in a fixed precessional position. The standard children's spinning top fails to do this and so makes it difficult to measure the values of a, b and c.

Questions

1. Make ω the subject of the equation.
2. If $v = 2$ what is ω in your gyroscope?
3. If $v = 0.5$ what is ω?
4. How are v and ω affected by changes in c?
5. How are v and ω affected by changes in a?

The Tippe Top

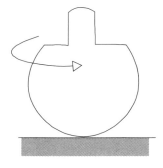

Other toys have gyroscopic motion; one of these is called the Tippe Top. This toy consists of a spherical body and a stem. The centre of gravity of the top is below the centre of curvature of the spherical body. If the Tippe Top is given sufficient spin it will turn over and spin on its stem. The same behaviour, rising up on to the point, can also be found in rugby balls and hard-boiled eggs when they are spun off their points. Tippe Tops can bought from most toy shops.

The reason for the rise is due to a precession caused by the friction between the top and the ground. When does the top rise?

The equation of the Tippe Top is given by

$$\tfrac{1}{2}\omega_1^2 = \tfrac{1}{2}\omega_2^2 + gy + F$$

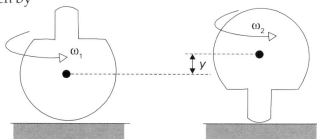

where ω_1 is the initial speed of spin, ω_2 is the speed of spin after it has turned over, y is the rise of the centre of gravity and F is the loss of energy due to friction.

Questions

1. Make ω_2^2 the subject of the equation.
2. Make F the subject of the equation.
3. Given that $\omega_2 = 3$, $g = 10$, $y = 0.02$ and $F = 3.3$, find the value of ω_1.
4. Using the above values for g, y and F, state the condition for the top to spin on its stem.

Rolling coin

One of the simplest types of gyroscopic motion is seen in a rolling coin. When a 10p coin or other such circular disc is rolled on a flat surface, its path becomes a spiral. This is due to the fact that it is difficult to roll a coin in an exact vertical orientation. As a result of the coin rolling slightly out of the vertical plane, its weight will cause it to precess in towards the centre of a spiral. I first noticed this when I was playing with one of my children a few years ago. As I rolled a doughnut-shaped plastic ring towards him, with roughly the same speed each time, he would try to catch it. After repeating this experiment a number of times, I noticed that the doughnuts seemed to be ending up in approximately the same place each time. After some calculations I worked out the reason for this. A by-product that I discovered was a way to find the initial speed and coefficient of friction of the surface by only measuring two values from this experiment.

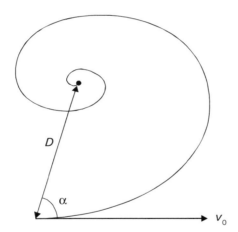

The two measurements you need to make are:

- the distance D between the start and finish positions
- the angle α between its initial speed direction v_0, and its final position.

Then you can use the following equation to find the coefficient of friction μ:

$$\tan \alpha = \frac{d}{3R\mu}$$

where R is the radius of the coin or disc and d is the distance the coin slants away from the vertical.

This slant distance can be difficult to calculate. I have found that it is best to roll the coin from a slanted wedge. This then allows you a means of calculating an exact value of d.

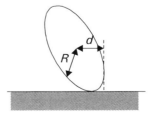

To find the initial speed v_0 of the coin, use the equation

$$2gD = \frac{3Rv_0^2}{\sqrt{d^2 + 9R^2\mu^2}}$$

taking $g = 10$, as before. You now have an approximate means of finding the coefficient of friction μ of any surface. By rolling the coin on various surfaces students will be able to compare their relative roughness. As with all the other toys in this chapter, you can get students to rearrange the formulas to make different variables the subjects of the equation. A good challenge with the above equation is to make μ the subject.

Further references

Crabtree, H. (1967) *An Elementary Treatment of the Theory of Spinning Tops and Gyroscopic Motion*, 3rd edn. New York: Chelsea Publishing Company.

Edge, R. D. (1987) *String and Sticky Tape Experiments*. College Park, MD: American Association of Physics Teachers.

Gray, A. (1918) *A Treatise on Gyrostatics and Rotational Motion*. New York: Dover (reprinted 1959).

Humble, S. (2001) 'Rolling and spinning coin', *Teaching Mathematics* **20**(1), 18–24 (also at www.teamat.oupjournals.org).

Perry, J. (1929) *Spinning Tops*. London: Sheldon Press.

Scheck, F. (1994) *Mechanics*, 2nd edn. Heidelberg: Springer Verlag.

See also:
www.toycrafter.com
www.pass.maths.org.uk/issue7/features/gyroscopes

Z Zoo Time with Tigers and Sea Shells

Have you ever wondered, walking around a zoo perhaps, why some creatures are stripy and others are spotty? If there were some sort of division in nature and we only had spotty or stripy beasts then maybe I would feel happier. Yet this is far from the case, since you can find animals with both stripes and spots and animals with neither. These markings also contain all manner of colours mixed into the overall pattern on the skin. I have only to look at my wife's beautifully freckled face to see a pattern that exists in such a random order that I could not hope to write down its mathematical formula. Or could I?

Alan Turing (see Chapter C) was a British mathematician who had a great many mathematical interests, one of which was the markings of animals. His hypothesis was that the surface of the embryo contained various chemicals which would compete for space as it grew. Turing thought that our genes sent out signals to these surface chemicals, which in turn formed patterns on our skin. Biologists became very excited about this idea and tested out Turing's equations, but unfortunately the equations failed to agree with the experiments.

Turing was working on animal markings in the 1950s, but in 1987 the work of a mathematical biologist called Professor Hans Meinhardt renewed interest in these ideas. He has proved that nearly all the markings on sea shells can be explained by equations similar to Turing's.

My interest in these patterns began with a dinner in an Italian restaurant. During the meal I found a shell with a pattern consisting of red lines arranged like nested W's. Since I had worked for a long time on the problem of biological pattern formation, this pattern caught my interest . . .

British mathematician Alan Turing (1912–1954)

125

He worked on these patterns and eventually found that nearly all sea shells throughout the world can be replicated with non-linear partial differential equations. These equations can simulate the battle which is fought out on the skin surface, between activators trying to put down colour, and inhibitors trying to stop it.

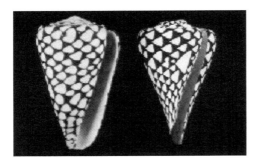 

You may be thinking that not all skins in one species are the same, and on some animals they are very different. Meinhardt explains this:

> *a traumatic event must have happened in the young animal's history such as temporary dryness, lack of food, or injury by a predator. After such a perturbation the pattern may be very different . . . yet by making adjustments to my model it is able to take account of such pattern irregularity.*

Even with his great insight into the pattern formation, he has to admit that there is very little understanding of the mechanisms involved, and no information at present can be obtained about the nature of the chemical substances which take part in this battle. It is an active research field and one in which there are no boundaries to stop the young experimenter. So it is a fitting place to end this personal tour of the A–Z of mathematics.

Experiment time

First it is important for students to collect and group into categories different types of animal markings. To start this activity, they need a collection of pictures. There are many ways to create this collection, including:

- A trip to the school library to collect pictures.
- A homework to bring in a book with animal pictures – every home will have something. Over the years I have seen a wonderful collection of books.
- Surfing the Internet.

Then consider the patterns.

- In pictures of tigers, students need to look for patterns, such as numbers of stripes on the old and young. Are the stripes on the face always symmetrical?
- If you are looking at giraffes, do the spots form three-, four- or five-sided shapes? Are these shapes uniform throughout the body?
- No zebra has the same face markings. Check to see if this is true.
- A jaguar is an example of a two-colour activator–inhibitor system. In other words, its skin is made up of three colours: one is the background, the inhibitor, and the other two activate the pattern on the skin.
- Dalmatian dogs have a crazy random pattern on their skin. Can you see an underlying order?
- The ordered spots of ladybirds, moths and angelfish produce good logical patterns.
- Meinhardt sea shells, some of which can be collected from the local beach or a bathroom shelf, if parents allow, are covered in wonderful patterns.

Once the students have collected and organised various animal patterns they can then start to experiment with the computer program ZOO. This program simulates one of the many sets of equations that are possible.

$$\frac{\partial a}{\partial t} = \frac{sbw}{s_b + s_c c} - r_a a + d_a \frac{\partial^2 a}{\partial x^2}$$

$$\frac{\partial b}{\partial t} = b_b - \frac{sbw}{s_b + s_c c} - r_b b + d_b \frac{\partial^2 b}{\partial x^2}$$

$$\frac{\partial c}{\partial t} = r_c (a - c) + d_c \frac{\partial^2 c}{\partial x^2}$$

The equations describing the patterns on the skin are very complex, and even mathematics professors have problems solving them. In fact, they cannot solve most of them without using a computer, and even then can only find approximate solutions depending on the quality of the algorithm they use. Each slightly different type of equation holds new problems for the adventurous solver.

A basic idea behind the sets of equations is that as one chemical grows in strength to become dominant, this will be the colour we see on the skin. Yet this dominance may not be constant, and with time a rival chemical will take over and so be the new colour or pair of colours, such as with jaguars. So the equations could be set up to grow this sort of imitation skin, as seen below.

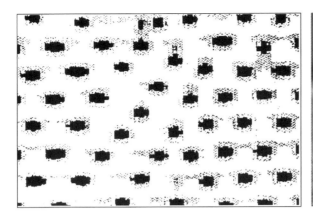 

The equations are given to illustrate where the constants and variables appear. When students start to change these numbers they will be able to relate this back to the equations, to see which part of the activator or inhibitor it comes from.

Computer support

First try running the program ZOO. You will see three colours: blue, green and red. These are the three variables a, b and c in the equations. Green is the inhibitor, or the basic background skin colour. In the program it is the letter B. Red is another inhibitor offering a second skin colour if required. It is the letter C. Blue is the activator, the skin colour causing spots or stripes. It is the letter A.

You can remove any of these from the screen printout by using REM at the start of the line. The program will still do all the calculations, but won't show this colour. For example, to omit the red change line 620 from

```
620 IF (((C(k) - B(k))>0) AND (C(k) - A(k)>0) THEN PSET(q,k),4
```

to

```
REM 620 IF (((C(k) - B(k))>0) AND (C(k) - A(k))>0) THEN PSET(q,k),4
```

The initial sites or initial conditions for the growth of colour are given in lines 210–380. All sites start as green apart from the four blue and four red sites given by the following lines. The '1' indicates the level of concentration of that colour. Try increasing these to other values to see the effect.

```
270 A(10)=1
280 A(22)=1
290 A(S5)=1
300 A(75)=1
350 C(5)=1
360 C(15)=1
370 C(35)=1
380 C(65)=1
```

Another change that can be made to these is their position, which is indicated by the number inside the brackets. So the blues are seeded at 10, 22, 55 and 75. You could change these to 2, 6, 10 and 14 – in other words cluster them at one end. Try this to see the effect.

At present there are only four seed points for blue and red, but in this program you could have up to 100. To add more simply type them in. For example:

```
271 A(11)=1
272 A(12)=1
273 A(14)=1
274 A(15)=1
275 A(18)=1
276 A(20)=1
```

This gives.you six more initial seed points. The effects are clear when you run the program. If you also change line

```
150 s=.08
```

to

```
150 s=.05
```

leaving in the above extra seed points, you will see some zebra stripes.

By changing s in line 150 you have started to experiment with the parameters in the equations:

```
80    h =.1
90    sa=.1
100   sb=1
110   sc=1.1
120   ra=.08
130   rb=.005
140   rc=.02
150   s=.05
160   ba=0.001
170   bb=.1
180   da=.01
190   db=0.02
200   dc=.4
```

These lines are very important to pattern formation. Slight changes in these will cause great changes in the picture you see on the screen.

- Begin with bb. This is in the second equation as b_b and plays an important role in the generation of inhibiting skin colour. Reduce it down to 0.01 and then gradually, increase it through the values 0.09, 0.095, 0.099, 0.105, 0.111 and 0. 115, checking the effect of each. You will see a pattern of stripes that wiggle then break up.
- The parameter given by line

```
150  s =.08
```

has catastrophic effects on the colour. Starting at 0.05, increase through to 0.4 to see its effect.

- By increasing the parameter given by line

```
160  ba=.001
```

to 0.05 you will see a periodic pattern of varying thickness in stripes.

In these cases only one of the parameters was altered at any one time. This is the safe way to start experimenting to get a feel for the whole set of equations. Once you have done this you can try changing pairs of parameters and then groups of three and more. The equations will give a diversity only limited by your enthusiasm. The challenge I set students is to find as many different possible animal skins as they can. Be warned. You must tell them to be systematic and keep clear notes on the changes they make to the program. It is very easy to find something wonderful and lose it by not writing down the change that was made.

Further references

Goodwin, B. (1994) *How the Leopard Changed its Spots: The Evolution of Complexity*. London: Weidenfeld & Nicolson.
Gordon, N. (1990) *Seashells: A Photographic Celebration*. New York: Friedman Group.
Kaandorp, A. J. (1994) *Fractal Modeling: Growth and Form in Biology*. New York: Springer.
Meinhardt, H. (1998) *The Algorithmic Beauty of Sea Shells*. Berlin: Springer Verlag.
Murray, J. D. (1993) *Mathematical Biology*. New York: Springer Verlag.

See also:
www.beloit.edu/~biology/shells
www.webdirectory.com
www.planetark.org
www.24hourmuseum.org.uk
www.britannica.com

Links to the National Curriculum

	Ma2 Number and algebra	Ma3 Shape, space and measures	Ma4 Handling data	ICT
A	•			
B		•	•	•
C	•	•		
D		•	•	
E		•		
F	•		•	•
G			•	
H	•			•
I	•		•	
J		•		•
K		•		
L	•	•	•	•
M	•		•	
N	•		•	
O	•	•		•
P	•	•	•	•
Q	•	•	•	
R	•			•
S	•			
T	•			•
U	•	•		
V			•	•
W	•			•
X	•	•	•	•
Y	•			
Z		•	•	•

Index

References to programs on the CD-ROM